The A–Z of Visual Ideas
How to Solve Any Creative Brief

John Ingledew

Laurence King Publishing

LAURENCE KING

Published in 2011 by Laurence King Publishing Ltd
361-373 City Road
London EC1V 1LR
United Kingdom
Tel: +44 20 7841 6900
Fax: +44 20 7841 6910
e-mail: enquiries@laurenceking.com
www.laurenceking.com

Reprinted 2012, 2013, 2014

A catalogue record for this book is available
from the British Library.

ISBN: 978-1-85669-714-9

Design: Studio Ten and a Half
Cover design: Jon Allan
Senior editor: Peter Jones
Printed in China

The A–Z of Visual Ideas
How to Solve Any Creative Brief

Contents

Introduction
What's the big idea?

The A–Z of Visual Ideas *aims to open doors that lead to adventures in the land of imagination and inspiration. It links and interconnects ideas from all creative disciplines and different periods of history, to explain how and why they work and help readers connect to numerous sources that will inspire them.*

The book is structured in an easy-to-use A–Z format. Each entry is a potential starting point for creating an idea or a possible source of inspiration to fire the imagination. It aims to help unlock creativity, ensuring that readers never again have to stare at a blank sheet of paper or a blank screen when striving for ideas. It aims to be an essential guide to creativity that will stimulate readers to create great work.

Ideas in the commercial arena need to provide answers to a client's problems, while ideas in art need to ask questions of the viewer. This book aims to provide stimulus, strategies and sparking points to create ideas that can both provide answers and ask provocative questions.

Entries in the A–Z section of the book have been chosen for their dominance in creativity and each one introduces a source of fertile inspiration or potential ideas. The ways in which an idea is able to seize the imagination and 'brainjack' a viewer is discussed and a 'how to' section that explains ways to explore it further is also included. Feed and develop your imagination with all the many different ideas discussed in the A–Z, be inspired by them – then transform this inspiration into ideas of your own.

Free creativity and ideas

Creativity was once highly compartmentalized with creative individuals pigeonholed within narrow roles – as artists, graphic designers, illustrators, typographers, photographers, film-makers, writers, musicians, directors, magazine designers, exhibition designers, product designers, interior designers, costume designers, retail designers, set designers, etc.

This strict demarcation has now dissolved and creative people can work freely across all these exciting disciplines. To do this successfully they need to be multitalented, multiskilled and totally multidisciplinary in outlook.

Though the ways in which they are able to work have changed radically the universal factor in what they do has not: all creativity needs great ideas.

What are ideas?
An idea is a sudden mental picturing of possibility – the realization that there is a possible way of doing something.

Communication

It is said that the motivation of all human creativity is the desire to communicate. This means both 'to have an interchange of thoughts or knowledge between people' and 'to have or to form a connection'. Communication is therefore exchanging information and forming connections with people – and is fundamental to creativity in both art and the commercial world.

Designer and writer Henry Wolf summed up this process as 'the difficult business of getting messages out of one mind into another'.

It is difficult, but also thrilling and hugely rewarding to communicate successfully and this book aims to show you the many ways in which you can do this.

Communication in art and commerce
A work of art aims to communicate the ideas of the person who created it whereas in commercial creativity the ideas need to communicate successfully on behalf of someone else: a client.

The challenge of communicating
You will seldom have a willing audience when you begin the task of communicating. You will have no volunteers queuing up expectantly to look at your work.

'Ideas are the content, execution is the style.'
Alan Smithee, designer

'You simply can't avoid a great idea.'
Schway Whar, designer

'It's thrilling that an idea you've created in your head can explode like fireworks in the heads of others.'
Rose Tang, artist

'When a brilliant idea connects to a viewer it's like a tenpin bowling "strike". It would be great if it made that noise too.'
Schway Whar, designer

The joy of communication
Coming up with a great idea is hugely satisfying. Encountering a great idea is equally enjoyable.

'A great idea draws your mental picture in the minds of other people.'
Rose Tang, artist

'Hang on a minute lads, I've got a great idea.'"
Michael Caine in *The Italian Job*, screenplay by Troy Kennedy Martin

Communication courses
People who worked creatively in design, advertising and illustration were once called commercial artists – encapsulating the fact that they were making creative work for commercial purposes.

When art colleges began to offer training for careers in commercial art the courses were in what was known as 'graphic design'. They are now often called 'visual communication', 'communication design' or simply 'communication' courses. 'Communication' is the best title so far, as it reflects that the aim of the course is to train students to get messages successfully into the minds of other people.

How can you engage these passers-by?

1. Switch the viewer's mindset
Create ideas that switch the viewer's mindset from off to on, from passive to active – thereby making them receptive to the message you want them to receive.

2. Ambush
Clearly communicating a message is not simply a matter of creating visually striking images that capture the eye of the viewer; it's about capturing their brain. You must create ideas that ambush their mind and thoughts, and execute these ideas in fresh and exciting visual ways.

3. Brainjack
You must strive to engage as powerfully as possible in order to communicate. The more potent the idea, the better the message will be remembered. The challenge is to create ideas that immediately grab the viewers' imaginations, light up their minds, create a joyful or jarring engagement, stimulate thoughts, emotions or action. You've got to brainjack the viewer. Doing this triggers a mental reaction such as an inner smile; additionally, it can provoke a physical reaction – such as a laugh or exhalation.

How different ideas brainjack successfully is discussed throughout this book.

Brainjack *v.* **1.** to communicate by seizing someone's imagination. **2.** to transmit or reveal information, feelings, emotions or thoughts so that they are clearly understood.

Ideas – a meeting of minds

In a meeting of minds between the creator of an idea and his or her audience there is a process of interaction and feeling of inclusion when the idea engages with the viewer's imagination. This bond occurs when the viewer recognizes, connects to and understands what the creator has set out to communicate because the connection in their mind is similar to the one that took place in the creator's imagination when he or she formed the idea.

Multidisciplinary designer Ross Cooper described what happens: 'When a viewer understands an idea they feel good about it. There's that moment when they "get it" in their mind, they feel they've done something clever, it brings out a smile. They feel good and feel a warmth at being included with the creator.'

Creativity is child's play

Children all over the world play a version of the transformation drawing game (*see* above). Working in pairs, one child draws a shape without really thinking about it, then the other transforms this abstract form into something recognizable. A triangle becomes a boat, a circle a face, a rectangle a house, etc. Writer and children's laureate Anthony Browne concluded that, 'Although on one level it's just a game, I believe it encapsulates the act of creation'. An inspiration is transformed by an idea into something new; creativity is as simple as this. This book examines the many ways in which ideas can transform inspiration.

'It is the most brilliant thing we do to have ideas. Anyone can have ideas, you don't need any equipment and your idea can change the world.'
John Hegarty, adman

Playful ideas

As children we create hugely inventive worlds during play. The scale and form of objects are happily ignored and overthrown. A stick is a knight's sword or a Jedi's glowing light sabre, a dressing-up box full of old clothes is the source of costumes from all nations and eras. At the seaside, while adults pursue a suntan, children build magnificent castles with towering turrets, drawbridges and moats fed by intricate waterways. They write imaginatively and draw wonderfully as is seen on refrigerators in every family home. As children, our imaginations are so powerful that we can even invent companions: imaginary friends.

The creative individuals whose work is showcased in this book are united by the fact that they have retained a spirit of childlike purpose and playfulness with objects, images, scale and words. Bring a child-like enthusiasm to what you do, sprinkle delight on it and be hugely playful with the ideas in this book.

'The photographer must look with the eyes of a child who sees the world for the first time.'
Bill Brandt, photographer

'What kinds of people know how to communicate? ... I think they are people who have managed to retain their infantile directness, who have resisted the crippling effects of education.'
Leo Rosten, writer

'Hopefully I have a very child-like view of the world.'
Paul Smith, designer

The brain: the storehouse of inspiration

Our brains are the storehouses of our lives. Recent experiences and discoveries are freshly stored while others are tucked away in dark recesses. Everything is a possible source of inspiration.

Inspiration: stimulus for the imagination

The word inspiration derives from the Latin *inspirare* (to breathe life into). Inspiration is the force that stimulates our imaginations to think creatively and have ideas, and breathes life into these ideas. This book offers many different ways in which to be inspired.

*'You should as a creative person constantly experience as much
as you can so that when a brief comes you've got some inspiration
already. The whole world gives you stuff to call on. Immerse
yourself in the world of culture – both high and low.'*
Liam Gibson, art director

The imagination: the brain's creative studio

The imagination is the part of the mind where ideas are
sparked and received, to transform inspiration into
something new. It is where creative ideas are conjured
up, and should be the place that all creative messages are
aimed. Targeting the viewer's imagination is the secret
of brainjacking. Our imaginations need to be constantly
fed with inspiration to help create fresh ideas. This book
aims to greatly nourish your imagination.

*'If you could look inside my imagination when I'm coming up
with ideas I think it would look like lots of popcorn popping.'*
Liam Gibson, art director

How does your creative imagination work?

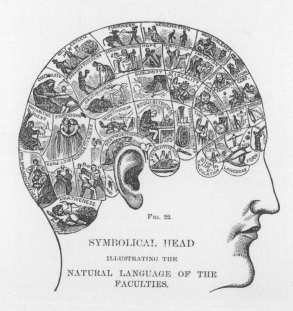

FIG. 22.

SYMBOLICAL HEAD

ILLUSTRATING THE

NATURAL LANGUAGE OF THE
FACULTIES.

The world inside our heads

The world inside our heads was perfectly visualized in a
recent exhibition at London's Hayward Gallery for which
a group of artists was challenged to produce installations
that show how the mind works.

Swiss artist Thomas Hirschhorn created a labyrinthine
series of caves with interlinking tunnels. Visitors walked
through winding passageways and caverns, the walls and
roofs of which were plastered with magazine articles,
random news pictures, film and pop music posters, pin-ups
and photocopied scraps; television screens sunk into the
walls flickered with long-forgotten programmes. Books,
some massively enlarged in scale, were piled high on shelves.
Some corners were dark and inaccessible. Hirschhorn
wrote: 'We think there's no light on them, we think they're
forgotten but they are not.' Everything was interconnected;
in every corner chaotic wiring was linked with small
explosive charges, all set to be detonated and remix and
reconnect the stored material in new ways. It was a messy
collage of memories, knowledge and desires, ready to
be triggered.

American artist Jason Rhoades exhibited piles of logs
stacked as if ready for the sawmill and covered with
random collections of images and information. Some
logs were already sawn, chopped in strange ways that
created new juxtapositions and chunks. Creative fuel
ready to fire the imagination. Neuroscience professor
Sophie Scott commented that Rhoades' work neatly
expressed the 'current thinking in neuroscience about
the way the frontal lobes are involved in creative thought'.

Chiharu Shiota from Japan created an installation
that featured miles of wool strung together to create
complex, interrelating patterns and connections. Professor
Scott wrote that, 'It was as if she'd stripped away all the
gunk and blood and tissue – and you were actually standing
in her brain.'

Ideas people

'In the colour spectrum of human endeavour, there are those at the indigo end who wish that everything would last forever. And then there are those opposite at the bright red end who believe that a day without 97 fresh ideas is a day without sunshine.'
Eve Babitz, writer

Great ideas people are polymaths, hugely interested in a massive range of subjects. They are Renaissance men and women, constantly open to inspiration with a huge desire to know about everything and anything. Ideas people are possessed by passion for people, knowledge and the world around us, and have great enthusiasm – the word itself derives from the Greek *entheos* (full of god, or possessed).

Ideas people flow round problems
Creative people are said to have the Protean gene – a reference to Proteus, a Greek god whose ability to become liquid enabled him to flow round any obstacle.

'Surprise me! Astonish me!'
Ideas people are rarely isolationists and most of them share their creative problems with collaborators who act as sounding boards and filters for their ideas. The Russian ballet impresario Sergei Diaghilev asked his colleagues to 'Surprise me!' while art director Alexey Brodovitch told the people he worked with to 'Astonish me!' The joy of all creative collaborations is finding creative playmates.

Creative double acts
Advertising agencies believe in pairs of collaborators, when an art director and a copywriter are coupled to bounce

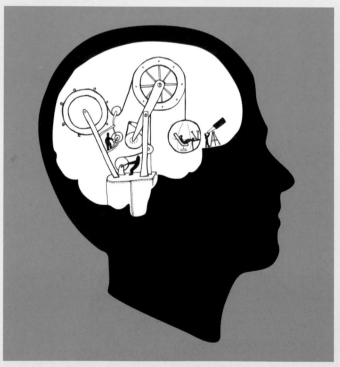

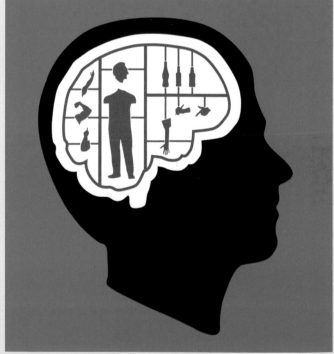

The world inside (below)
Asked to design posters for a series of talks
by idearists, Kirsty Pook imagined the world
inside each speaker's head.

ideas off each other. Initial ideas can be fragile and having a partner whom you trust totally means your wildest thoughts can be voiced without fear of ridicule or knock-back. An exciting creative telepathy can be engendered in a partnership.

Creative double acts are seen in many mediums. Examples are photographers Pierre et Gilles (*see* Places of worship) artists Gilbert and George, and comedians Laurel and Hardy, Morecambe and Wise, and the Two Ronnies (*see* Wordplay). Other partnerships include Rogers and Hammerstein, and Lennon and McCartney in the music business, and, in the movies, Powell and Pressburger,

'In a partnership you have to convince the other person that what you are doing is good.'
Rebecca Brown and Mike Heath, multidisciplinary designers

Try working with both like-minded and unlike-minded people. They will challenge you in different ways.

Enthusiasm is contagious, so find enthusiastic collaborators. Work with people who are possessed by passion, who stimulate you, make you laugh, challenge you, who you trust and with whom you spark.

Undertake collaborations with people from many creative disciplines, and learn from the cross-fertilization of ideas and working methods.

Idearists

Idearists have a hunger for information and a thirst for knowledge. Idearists are rule-breakers, rewriters of rules, rule-haters, risk-takers, tide-turners, table-turners, game-changers, goal-post movers and match-winners. They are questioning, provocative and versatile. Idearists are

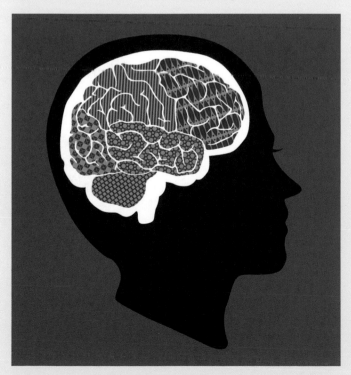

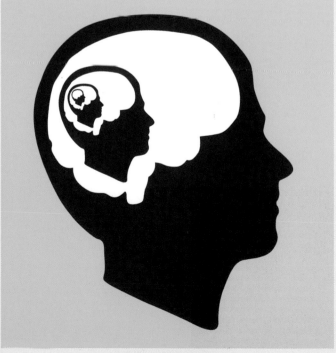

ingenious improvisers who do the unexpected, turn things around and are spontaneous, dogged, obsessive and obsessional. They have a great sense of humour and sense of the absurd. Idearists are curious; they are observers, fascinated by people and things. Idearists possess open minds, they think big, are freethinkers, forward thinkers. They think without a safety net, they make others think, they turn you on, they don't switch off, they don't watch the clock; they're always switched on, they live for their work. Idearists are visionary.

'There's no off position on the genius switch.'
Danny Baker, broadcaster

The language of creativity and ideas

A rich and revealing language is used to describe creativity and ideas. An idea is a 'conception', a word also used for the beginning of life. We 'give birth' to ideas indicating that creativity is a natural but sometimes painful process. An idea is the 'brainchild' of its creator, indicating that it needs careful nurturing. Ideas are also said to 'come to fruition' and 'bear fruit' – both natural processes.

Creative people are said to be able to 'think laterally'– 'look sideways' or 'at a tangent'– and have the ability to 'turn problems on their heads', all of which communicates their capacity to see the world from different perspectives and highly unusual angles. Ideas come from the brain and link to the intelligence of the viewer. A poor idea is described as being 'half brained', indicating it has not been wholly formed in the mind of its creator. In France a poor idea is described as a 'wet fire cracker'.

In the joyous world of the children's comics of the 1950s and 1960s, when a character had a great idea it was often described as a 'wizard wheeze'. This perhaps derives from the exhalation of breath that can occur when someone understands an idea – the expression comically suggests that this causes a cheery, whistling sound. Equally quaint is the concept of someone 'putting their thinking cap on' to generate ideas.

Like Proteus, creativity is sometimes seen as a liquid – for example, in the concept of 'getting creative juices flowing' in order to solve a problem, and in the way ideas are said to 'brew' or 'percolate' in the mind. They are also described as 'brainwaves' and the brain as a 'think tank'. A highly creative person offers a 'torrent' of great ideas.

Being 'struck by an idea' equates having ideas with conflict while a 'lightning flash of inspiration' and 'brainstorming' liken creativity to a tempest. 'A creative leap forward', 'a leap of the imagination', 'pushing the boundaries' and 'a ground-breaking idea' convey creativity as an energetic, physically demanding and challenging activity.

Ideas and their pursuit are often described as 'exploring' – or 'pushing' – 'the creative envelope'. These expressions became popular in the 1990s, and were most often used by non-creative people. Perhaps they are the

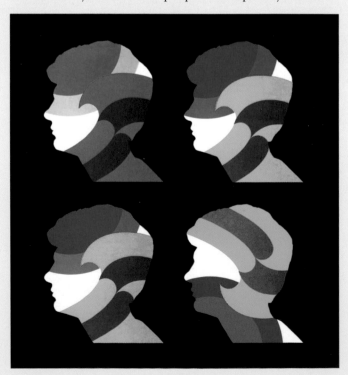

result of eureka-moment ideas being hastily scribbled on the backs of envelopes, in the absence of other pieces of blank paper. Sir Alec Issigonis is said to have designed the revolutionary Mini in this way. It has also been suggested that the expression comes from aviation – that the envelope is the structure that contained the gas for an airship – and refers to test pilots pushing aircraft to their furthest limit. Other up-in-the-air terms include 'blue sky' and 'clear sky' thinking.

Other languages and cultures also have terms for fresh and exciting ideas. In Italy they are referred to as 'third horizon thinking' and in France they have 'jumped from one river bank to another' while in China they are described as 'ideas that jump out of the frame'; in Brazil a fantastic idea is 'from the magician's top hat'.

Ideas about ideas

In his thought-provoking *The Act of Creation* Arthur Koestler puts forward the theory that the creative process 'consists in the discovery of hidden similarities'. He argues that this is the key to all the new ideas in visual creativity, science and humour.

Make linking jumps
Koestler concludes that innovative creative ideas result from the ability to make a linking jump from one frame of reference to another. This is achieved through understanding established patterns, codes of behaviour and types of logic, then breaking free from them to discover and reveal new connections or interrelationships.

This idea is reflected in the phrases 'jumped from one river bank to another', 'a leap of the imagination' and 'jump out of the frame'.

Derail the usual trains of thought
Koestler relates that breaking and undoing regular habits of thought is a key to ideas: 'The prerequisite of originality is the art of forgetting, at the proper moment, what we know… Without the art of forgetting, the mind clutters

with ready-made answers, and never finds occasion to ask the proper questions.'

Trying to forget or avoid normal patterns and habits of thought can be challenging. For example: Which of the following letters is the odd one out: A F H K M N Y Z? Normal habits and patterns of thought lead us to try to find a relationship between the letters. However, the odd one out is M. It is made from four straight lines, the others feature three. To solve the problem we have to forget we are looking at letters and and see them as lines.

Creativity as a paradox
Paradoxically, creative brains have to be simultaneously open to new ideas and focused on solving the problem at hand. It is necessary to hold two seemingly opposing requirements in the mind at precisely the same time.

The collective telepathic intelligence
There has been speculation that human beings possess a telepathic collective intelligence that allows them to enhance each other's wisdom without formal communication or interaction. Researchers have attempted to verify this phenomenon: they asked groups of individuals to complete a series of mental tasks then later asked new groups, totally unconnected to the first, to do the same. Results indicate that the latter groups had less difficulty performing the tasks, suggesting that collectively, as time passes, we could find problem solving increasingly easy.

Horizontal thoughts
It has been suggested that ideas solidify more readily when we are horizontal as more blood flows from the upper body to the brain. It is thought that when we are vertical the brain becomes less efficient at certain types of thinking.

Seeding ideas
Is it possible to seed the brain in the way that clouds can be seeded to produce rain, to make it more open to producing ideas? This book aims to seed the brains of its readers.

Strategies for solving a creative brief

In commercial creative work you are paid to find ways to communicate successfully with people. Your job is to ensure that your client's target audience 'gets the message' you've been employed to send.

Adman Raymond Chin said: 'The hardest thing is coming up with ideas in a pressure situation.' This book aims to help you do just this by discussing numerous sources of ideas and inspiration and, in this section, outlining actions to take at every stage of commercial creativity.

The process of communicating on behalf of a client and strategies for solving a brief can be broken down into 16 stages.

Writer and professor of philosophy A.C. Grayling encapsulated the skills needed to communicate when he wrote: 'The intellectual gifts are a capacity to see things from highly unusual angles, to overlook what is not essential, and to understand the true significance of the obvious. The character traits are persistence, obduracy, a capacity for taking great pains, and indifference to ridicule.'

Simplify at every stage

Simplify, don't complicate. You need to edit, pare down and chop away at every stage of solving a brief, from analyzing it to the final images you create. Reduce, cut the clutter, get to the essence, crop and cut out any irrelevance. Create simple ideas that expand in the viewer's imagination.

As adman John Hegarty pointed out: 'The French Revolution got its message down to only three words – *Liberté, Egalité, Fraternité.*' Likewise, the Chinese president Deng Xiaoping defined his ambitions for China in the words 'Reform and open'.

'You have to crop everything down to concentrate the viewer's mind. The more extraneous stuff there is, the more you lose sight of the idea.'
Clive Challis, art director and teacher

1

The briefing

The first stage is when you are given the brief – the assignment from a client that outlines the problem you are commissioned to solve creatively.

Clearly identify in discussions with the client what you are being asked to do. Simplify. What are you trying to achieve? What are the 'deliverables' – what have you been asked to deliver?

Be courageous. Ask the client all the questions that immediately come to mind, however stupid or innocent they may seem. The answers could totally turn the brief on its head. The barrier created by thinking 'I may make a fool of myself if I say this' could lead to great ideas remaining undiscovered.

They all laughed at Christopher Columbus
When he said the world was round
They all laughed when Edison recorded sound
They all laughed at Wilbur and his brother
When they said that man could fly
They told Marconi
Wireless was a phony
It's the same old cry…
…Who's got the last laugh now?
George Gershwin, composer

Don't be afraid to ask
When Kenneth Grange was asked to design British Rail's new intercity train a naive question came into his mind: 'What exactly are the buffers on a locomotive for?' He expected to be told, 'They're to stop trains crashing on to

Paddington station, stupid!' and was overjoyed to learn instead that their purpose was to shunt carriages – an unnecessary hangover from a bygone age. Freed of the need to include buffers, he could design a streamlined train that attained previously unheard-of speeds and thereby revolutionized rail travel in Britain.

Ask childlike questions
Edwin Land was inspired to design the revolutionary, instant-photograph Polaroid camera in the 1940s when his three-year-old daughter asked, 'Why can't I see the pictures now?'. Similarly writer Roger Hargreaves began writing his million-selling *Mr Men* books after his young son asked, 'What does a tickle look like?'

2

Analyze the challenge

Fiercely unpick the brief. Read, read and then reread it. Clearly identify in your own mind what the client needs. What is the goal you are asked to achieve?

Question and requestion the brief. Get to the essence of the problem you have to solve. Philosopher John Dewey said 'A problem well stated is half-solved'. Simplify the problem so that it is clearly stated. Ask yourself: What is the purpose of the brief? What is the message I have been asked to send and who are the people I am asked to send it to? What is the standpoint? What is my client's need?

The result of this stage should be that you are clear about the challenge the brief poses.

And, of course, consider the deadline.

'The anchor to a great solution is totally understanding a brief.'
Nick Hastings, creative director

'Find what is at the heart of a brief, find truths and fundamentals, things that are unique and undeniable about it.'
Schway Whar, designer

'The first thing I do is try to really understand what the brief is. We try to simplify and hone it down to its essential words. This really helps you to focus. We're currently working on a ten-page brief which we've been able to get down to 15 words.'
Jon Mitchell, art director

'When we get a brief we really try to distil it to the one thing we need to do. Briefs are often overwritten. We try to get really clear. As a team we try to get to a "truth" about the brief that we find irrefutable, that we can't really argue with.'
Georg Thesmann, art director

'I break a brief down into simple bullet points. We then pull together moodboards for the project, the look, the feel and the palette of the project. We surround ourselves with the world of the client, from books and from the internet. We educate ourselves about the client. When we have got that together we use these images as our sparks for ideas.'
Alan Aboud, art director

3

First ideas

Collate all the first thoughts about the brief that come into your head.
What do your instincts tell you to do? What are your 'reflex' ideas?
Develop your intuitive response to the brief.

Use this book to help you to inspire your first ideas.

'One in a hundred times your first idea will be utterly brilliant – the other 99 times ideas will come from really getting under the skin of the brief and the audience.'
Nick Hastings, creative director

4

Visualization

Visualization is the process of putting your ideas down on paper.

Make your first thoughts visual. Always visualize your ideas immediately – doodle, draw and sketch. Use this book to inspire your visualization. By making things visual you can 'push' initial ideas by sparking new thoughts and finding new connections.

'Pour all your thoughts and ideas on to a page no matter how half-formed they are. You can then look at them as a whole. Visualization allows you to begin to make new connections between things.'
Ross Cooper, multidisciplinary designer

Learn different ways to visualize ideas
Picture in your imagination the drawings and illustrations from the books of your childhood that you have stored in your mind. Assess and evaluate why these particular visualizations of ideas have been stored so successfully. Be inspired by doing this. *See* You! (put yourself in it).

Learn from great visualizers of ideas: James Gillray and George Cruikshank (*see* Caricature), Aubrey

Beardsley, Saul Steinberg, George Grosz, Gerard Hofnung, William Heath-Robinson and Shigeo Fukada (*see* Illusion, Shadows). These creative people have no boundaries when they visualize ideas and are hugely playful with scale, words, visual metaphors and visual coincidences.

See the storyboards that creators of television advertisements and movie-makers such as Terry Gilliam and Tim Burton draw to visualize their ideas. These are created in order to fine-tune concepts and maximize the impact of what will be filmed.

5

Know the subject / know the product

Now do your homework. Get to know the subject of the brief. Go on investigative fact-finding missions. Gather all the facts. Experience the product if you can. Interview. Be sociable; talk to people about the problem you have been asked to solve. Listen. Really get to the essence of the brief and become an authority on what it is all about.

'At this stage try going off at a tangent. If your brief is about a skin cream go talk to the guy that looks after the skin of an aircraft or a skyscraper, go talk to the guy at the zoo who looks after the skin of the elephants – these can lead to great insights.'
Phil Dorman, creative director

'When designing the cup and saucers for illy [see Mirror, Mirror] we did all our research into their previous designs, then we went for coffee in one of their cafés. Suddenly, rather than seeing the brief as designing two pieces of porcelain, we understood that we were creating something that was to do with an experience rather than objects: that coffee is served to you and you interact with the cup and saucers while you drink –

for example, you reveal the hidden circle on the saucer when lifting the cup and the coffee can be accidentally spilt. Getting to know our subject in this way led to our designs.'
Ross Cooper, multidisciplinary designer

At the end of this stage you should have a thorough knowledge of your subject.

6

Know your audience

When a stand-up comedian performs he or she must tailor their material to the audience. Nurses laugh at very different things to merchant bankers. You will nearly always be targeting a tough crowd, so always prepare. You need to create rapport and chemistry with every audience.

Graphic designer Derek Birdsall wrote that the key to great book design was 'simply putting oneself in the position of the reader,' commenting that 'it may seem common sense but it is surprisingly uncommon'.

Everyone has an appetite for ideas. The challenge for creative people is to create ideas that their viewers will want to consume.

'The only way of establishing a first entry is to understand what your audience knows.'
Milton Glaser, graphic designer

Put yourself in your viewers' shoes and try to inhabit their minds. Understand their hopes, their dreams and aspirations. Interview your audience – get insider knowledge. Find what will put them at their ease, what makes them laugh or what will shock them. Find out about their pageants, rites of passage, rituals, use of technology, secret pleasures and anxieties, their vocabulary, their music, television habits and the movies they love and hate. Evelyn Waugh wrote, 'The accumulation of common experience, private jokes and private language… lies at the foundation of English friendship.' Become friends with your audience by studying these things.

At the end of this stage you should have a thorough knowledge of your viewers.

7

Assimilate

Bring all your homework together.

You should now know about your subject and how to engage your audience. Mentally digest this information and break it down into its clearest and simplest elements.

8

Play with all you have learnt

This is the creative and fun part when you let the things that inspire you act as a catalyst to produce ideas. Creativity should be like child's play – truly pleasurable. This stage is when you put on your thinking cap, place your imagination in the front of your mind, put your brain in gear and let the creative juices flow!

In the previous stages you assembled your creative material. Now make links between what you know and what you have learnt. Seek previously undiscovered connections.

'Combinatory play seems to be the essential feature in productive thought.'
Albert Einstein, theoretical physicist

'The work you have done in the earlier stages has built a solid creative trampoline on which you can now bounce.'
Nick Hastings, creative director

'Without play there would be no Picasso. Without play there is no experimentation. Experimentation is the quest for answers.'
Paul Rand, designer

Review your knowledge and the discoveries you made in stages 6 and 7. Lay out all the information you have gathered about the creative problem and the audience. Now enjoy yourself with this information. Be imaginative – let your creative mind go to work – and go out to play.

This is the time to think laterally, sideways and tangentially, when you try to turn the problem on its head. Play and have fun with all the facts you have gathered. Put the pieces together in different ways.

Collage and make connections. Make free associations by recording your stream of consciousness – the random flow of thoughts that is triggered by a new situation.

Treat this stage like a game and fit unexpected pieces together. Try to discover coincidences both visual and verbal, seek previously unseen connections, relationships and associations between disconnected elements. Add to this mix the things that inspire you and use them to breathe life into your thoughts, to create ideas.

Additionally, now that you have the facts explore your intuitive and instinctive feelings once again. Adman Leo Burnett recommended: 'Steep yourself in your subject, work like hell, and love, honour and obey your hunches.'

Use the A–Z to be playful
Take inspiration from the A–Z section, and the strategies for playfulness given in the 'how to' information in every

entry – and transform what you have discovered about your brief and audience into visual and verbal ideas.

By the end of this stage you should have a pile of different concepts.

Keep playing, don't stop playing – and don't get rusty at the ideas game.

Stuck? Try these strategies
There are various tools to help the creative juices to flow again when thinking becomes tired, mired or at a dead end. Most of them will reconnect you to being playful.

1. Take a card, any card
In his teaching of lateral thinking Edward de Bono recommends picking a word at random from the dictionary as a catalyst to finding new connections.

Playing cards have also been used to stimulate thinking: each card features a cryptic remark or phrase, such as 'What would your best friend do?'– 'Now do the opposite!' or 'Amplify the most embarrassing details'. The cards are shuffled and drawn at random when someone is stuck or deadlocked. Sets have been evolved in advertising and design agencies, and some have been published commercially including a deck co-created by the musician Brian Eno.

2. Chance creation
Other ideas include cutting up and assembling snippets of unrelated text until they crystallize into understandable phrases that provide a fresh approach to a problem because they have been created by chance.

The author's strategy when he is stuck is 'fifth book along'. Go to a library to find a book related to your brief or project; then, as well as borrowing this book, take out the fifth one along from it on the shelf, in both directions – and also go five shelves up and down if possible. You will always find something inspiring in the additional books.

3. Sketchbooks
Refer to the store of ideas you already have in your sketchbooks and notebooks – rethink, adapt and evolve them. *See* Sketchbooks and scrapbooks.

4. Wait until the last minute!
A 'just in time' policy can create a pressured intensity of creativity that produces fresh thinking. However, this is not recommended as a first-choice strategy for solving every brief.

5. Use this book
Try randomly picking an entry from the A–Z section. Use it to help you generate ideas.

Still stuck? Try another entry.

Visualize further

Visualize the ideas you created in stage 7.

Review your first ideas in the light of the facts you found in stages 5 and 6.

Visually refine and simplify a range of developed ideas.

Incubation / reflection

Reflect on the ideas you have created. Judge them.

Are you communicating in a language your audience will understand? Examine each developed idea in the light of what you know about them. Will they really get it? Will it really connect with them?

Pick the best ideas. Eliminate any that on reflection don't work.

'Now get rid of the obvious stuff – reject the stuff that you think is not creative enough.'
Nick Hastings, creative director

11

Final visuals

Simplify further. The final execution of your ideas should put them in their most potent form. Be clear in your message – images should talk from 100 metres away.

12

Presentation / the pitch

Your final ideas will be presented, or pitched, to the client.

Prepare your presentation carefully. A pitch should be presented with clarity, confidence and pizzazz. Tell the story of how your design evolved clearly and simply, and refer to all the creative investigation you have done. Aim to be highly articulate. Express yourself, and deliver your

pitch, with passion and conviction. Many great ideas fall flat in front of clients because of poor presentation. Rehearse first and bring energy and enthusiasm to your pitch.

You must be persuasive. Hold out for your best ideas, and aim to convince the client that they will work. Make an impression – impress your ideas into the client's imagination.

13

Consensus

Come to an agreement with the client on which idea or ideas have cracked the brief.

14

Implementing the idea

This is the execution stage. Now bring your own signature to the idea. Follow writer George Eliot's advice: 'Do not go where the path may lead; go instead where there is no path and leave a trail.' *See* You! (put yourself in it).

The final execution is all about choosing the visual tone to express the idea. Find your look and make it yours. Make it individual. Make it your visual voice. Do you want to be exuberant, stylish, cool or complex? How the implementation of an idea is detailed is critical. Adman

John Hegarty describes this stage as 'like telling a joke: many different people can attempt to tell the same story but only one of them makes you really laugh – the delivery is key.'

Use this book to inspire how you deliver your ideas.

15

Deadline

The deadline, the time agreed for the delivery of your finished creative work, is usually fixed at the initial briefing. The word deadline comes from lines drawn on the ground over which captives were forbidden to pass on pain of death.

Hand over your final creative work to the client.

16

Publication and dissemination

Launch and distribute your ideas in the wider world in print, on the internet, on billboards, in magazines or by other means.

Use this book for inspiration about different ways of disseminating your work.

Working on ideas

A creative job is not one in which you clock in and off. Whereas most people have a clear delineation between work and non-work time this does not apply to ideas people. They are constantly absorbing inspiration and thinking about their projects or the briefs they are working on.

Twenty-four hour creativity

Creativity is a 24-hour-a-day process that involves periods of active pursuit and also 'unconscious' work, which takes place during times of relaxation; sleep seems to be as important as consciously striving for ideas.

Creative distraction

Ideas often solidify when we are not actively thinking. During a long soak in his bath Archimedes, the ancient Greek mathematician and inventor, suddenly leapt from the suds shouting 'Eureka!' (I've found it). He'd been struck by the perfect answer to a problem he'd been trying to solve.

The playful aspect of the creative process can be aided by engaging in a pleasurable and stimulating distraction. For Archimedes it was a bath, for Sherlock Holmes it was music. Advertising agencies often kit out their studios with pool tables and table football machines to provide an area in which to take breaks from active thinking and striving for answers. Creative distraction gives the brain free time to chew over partially formed ideas and allows the subconscious to work towards a synthesis – at a certain point something gels and solidifies as a firm idea.

Find the creative distractions that work for you. Listening to music or the radio, running, popping out for cigarettes, taking the dog for a walk, cycling, making tea and going to the movies (*see* Movies) are some of the distractions embraced by people who were interviewed for this book.

'You remember how Sherlock Holmes used to stop right in the middle of a case and drag Watson off to a concert? That was a very irritating procedure to the literal-minded Watson.'
James Webb Young, adman

'I get my best ideas in my car. In a car you can't do anything practical, so your thoughts start wandering off into a different

Brainwave (below)
Designer Kirsty Pook imagines the world
inside the author's head.

mode. It's as if I'm working on two levels; I'm driving and at the same time I am somewhere else. Working out how to solve a problem always happens in my car.'

Lotte Romer, musician and author, interviewed in *Inspired: How Creative People Think, Work and Find Inspiration*

'Stuff your conscious mind with information, then unhook your rational thought process. You can help this process by going for a long walk, or taking a hot bath, or drinking half a pint of claret. Suddenly, if the telephone line from your unconscious is open, a big idea wells up within you.'

David Ogilvy, adman

'Men of lofty genius when they are doing the least work are most active.'

Leonardo da Vinci, painter, scientist and engineer

Sleep on it

You can't solve a creative problem? Then sleep on it. Creativity is the only job you can do well while you are sleeping – but don't try billing your clients for the time. There is as much brain activity during sleep as while we are awake, and the sleeping brain can creatively rearrange our thoughts in perfect order and help us to find answers. As writer John Steinbeck put it: 'It is a common experience that a difficult problem at night is resolved in the morning after the committee of sleep has worked on it.'

Sherlock Holmes: 'Now I recommend the universal solution to all problems.'
Dr Watson: 'What's that, Holmes?'
Sherlock Holmes: 'Sleep!'

'You never have to change anything that you've got up in the middle of the night to write.'
Saul Bellow, writer

'We think that what's happening in sleep is that you open the aperture of memory and are able to see the bigger picture.'
Neuroscientist Matthew Walker, University of California, Berkeley

'At night while we are asleep our brains are secretly moonlighting for us.'
Rose Tang, artist

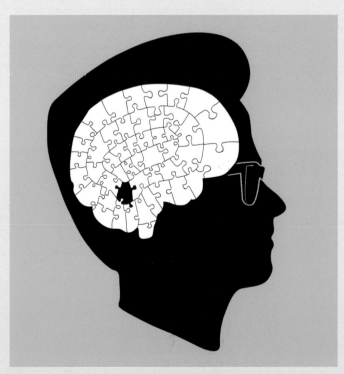

A

Art

A small number of priceless paintings hang in the art gallery that is in every person's mind. Leonardo da Vinci's Mona Lisa *and* Last Supper, *Munch's* The Scream, *Constable's* The Hay Wain *and van Gogh's* Sunflowers *are all there. We can picture them instantly. Ideas based on art can immediately grab the attention of the viewer.*

Ads for Habitat, 2006 (right and below)
London-based agency WDMP recreated three of the most famous paintings in London's National Gallery in this campaign for home store Habitat. Holbein's *The Ambassadors*, Van Eyck 's *The Arnolfini Marriage* and *Venus at Her Mirror* by Velázquez are recast with models echoing the profile of Habitat's customers and filled with their products to promote their new stock. Some symbols from the original paintings are wittily updated. *See* Symbols.

E. J. Major, *Venus Vanitas,* **2009 (opposite)**
Hong Kong-born artist E. J. Major reinterprets Velázquez's painting to make viewers think. Her work questions the representation of women in art, film and fashion magazines. The original was once attacked with an axe by a suffragette for representing women as vain, vacuous and self-absorbed in mirror-gazing. *See* Mirror, Mirror, www.ejmajor.co.uk

Inspiration from art galleries

Be inspired by visiting art galleries and art exhibitions. Get to know the history of art. Immerse yourself in the key art movements that have informed visual communication, including Pop Art, Surrealism, Constructivism and Dada. Try to see as many famous paintings and sculptures as you can rather than viewing them on the computer screen or in books, so that you can witness at first hand the original vision of the artist.

Study the origin and descent of ideas and inspiration through the history of art and design. Discover the interconnections and sources of inspiration of each art and design movement. The greatest designers and artists have always connected with the past to produce their most innovative work.

Investigate the historical cross-pollination and constant interplay between art and design. Sometimes designers appear to lead the artists; at other times they seem to follow them. Pop Art was inspired by the commercial designs of Coca-Cola bottles, Brillo boxes, Campbell's soup cans and Popeye and Dick Barton comic books. In turn, the work of the Pop artists inspired designers in numerous fields including interior design, industrial design, graphics, retail design, packaging and fashion.

Recomposing the past

The compositions of historical paintings can be used as inspiration. Their power, harmonies, rhythms and discords can have an immediacy and clarity that instantly connects to a viewer. Throughout creative history people have taken inspiration from their forebears by reinterpreting the visual construction of images from the past. Some of these reinterpretations go on to become the source material for work by later creative people as an ongoing cycle continues.

Take a broad brush approach

Be inspired not only by Western art but also the art and design of other cultures. For example, African art, Aboriginal art, Japanese art, Islamic art and South American art are all packed with surprising and inspirational ways of expressing ideas. *See* Maths.

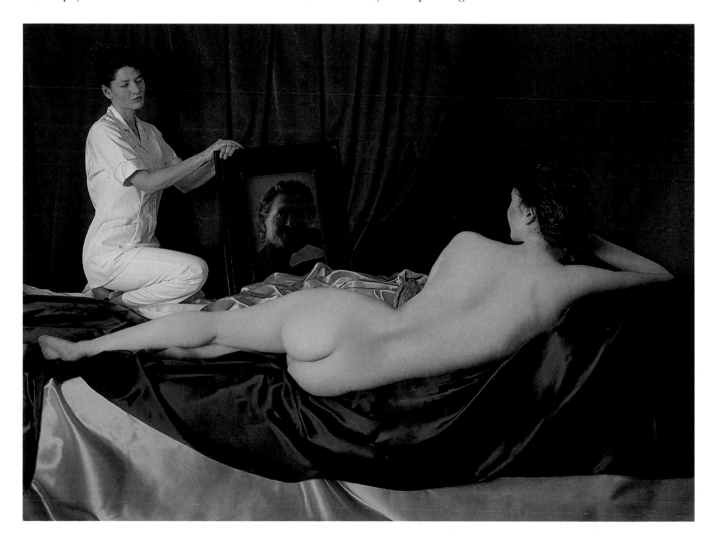

Fabrica, *Visions of Change*, 2001 (below left)
Young designers at Fabrica, the Benetton-sponsored design lab in Italy, created the exhibition Visions of Change in reaction to the 11th September 2001 attack in New York. Grant Wood's *American Gothic*, the painting reputed to be the most famous in America for its depiction of heartland American values, was updated for the exhibition.

Dick Jewell, *The Last Supper on the League Table*, 1988 (bottom)
Artist Jewell uses the composition of Leonardo's *Last Supper* in his celebration of the football World Cup.
See www.dickjewell.com

Red Saunders, *Thomas Paine*, from the *Hidden* series, 2009 (below right)
Saunders recreates important moments in the struggle of working people for democracy and social justice. 'History has been dominated by kings, queens, war and "great men". The Hidden series engages with a different historical narrative involving dissenters, revolutionaries and radicals.'

'As part of the process of finding inspiration for my photo series Hidden *I visited the National Gallery and Tate Britain in London and the Van Gogh Museum and Rijksmuseum in Amsterdam. The lighting in the paintings of Rembrandt, Caravaggio and van Gogh have always had a huge influence on a studio-trained photographer like myself. For* Thomas Paine *I studied the paintings of Joshua Reynolds, Stubbs and Gainsborough. For me, art galleries are a brilliant place to get my "palette" sorted out, research stuff; just stand in front of great works and let them spill all over you.'*

Red Saunders, artist, photographer, film-maker and activist

Tom Hunter, *The Way Home*, from *Life and Death in Hackney* series, 2000
English artist Hunter's intimate pictures of the young people of the East End of London take inspiration from famous paintings – using their compositions, lighting and gestures – in this case the source is the Pre-Raphaelite masterpiece *Ophelia* painted by John Everett Millais – which in turn had been inspired by Shakespeare's play *Hamlet*. In 2006 Hunter was the first artist to have a photography show at the National Gallery, London. *See* www.tomhunter.org

'I love paintings. All young people starting in the film business should study paintings... I used Rembrandt's lighting to light Marlene Dietrich.'

Jack Cardiff, cinematographer

DIY
Seek examples of famous artworks that connect to your brief of project in subject matter or content. Study the bloodlines of art history for inspiration.

Brainjack
When a viewer recognizes a deeply familiar painting in a surprising new context it triggers the question: 'I know this picture – what have they done here?' A feeling of visual *déjà vu* is created. Knowledge of the original painting – for example, its title, status or meaning – create an engaging interplay in the viewer's mind between the original and the re-creation. The more familiar the original, the more striking the new vision.

B

Building a bigger picture

An image built from a multitude of smaller elements is hugely arresting. The British photographer Arthur S. Mole created astonishing, giant images of American symbols, including the Liberty Bell and the Statue of Liberty made from photographs of up to 30,000 standing soldiers. Designers and artists have used everything from living flowers, Lego bricks and Rubik's cubes to coloured paint pots, mugs of tea of different strengths, and even cars as building materials.

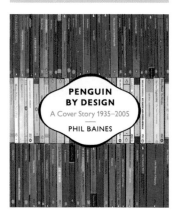

Ruth Adams, *1984* **book cover, 2006 (top)**
Cover design for George Orwell's 1948 novel about the oppressive Big Brother state – the tyrant's all-seeing eye is built from the faces of thousands of politicians' portraits. *See* www.ruthadams.co.uk.

David Pearson, *Penguin by Design* **book cover, 2005 (above)**
Pearson's cover for a book about the iconic cover designs of Penguin paperbacks is smartly created by using shelfloads of the books. *See* www.davidpearsondesign.com

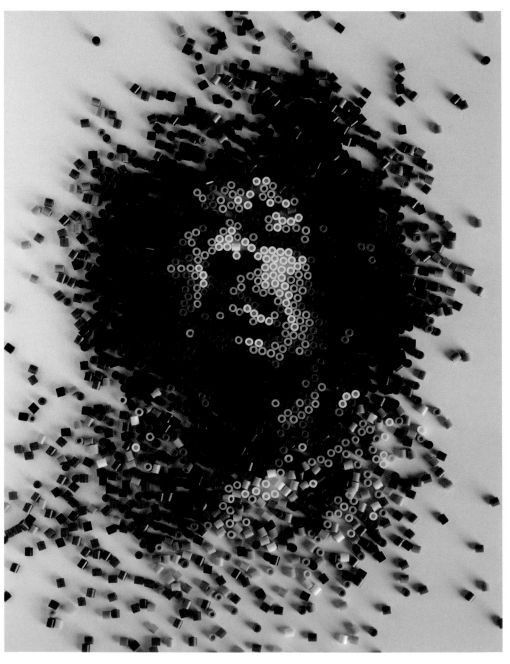

Ian Wright, *Experience Jimmy Hendrix*
(opposite)
English illustrator Ian Wright builds portraits
using hundreds, sometimes thousands of
similar small objects. He has built wonderful
pictures of musician Cheikh Lo from coloured
Lego bricks, Angela Davies from eyelash
curlers and Tony Bennett from souvenir
badges. Here he builds Jimmy Hendrix from
coloured beads. Wright's work has been
exhibited around the world. *See* Materials.

Arthur S. Mole, *The Human Liberty*
*Bell,***1918 (below left)**
One of a series of giant American symbols
created by Mole using servicemen returning
from the First World War. See Symbols.

Invader, *London Calling,* **2009 (bottom)**
The Parisian street artist Invader twists
hundreds of Rubik's cubes to rebuild his
favourite record album covers.

Marcus Harvey, *Myra,* **1995 (below right)**
Artist Harvey created one of the most
controversial paintings of the late 20th
century when he used stencils of children's
handprints to build this massive picture of
child-murderer Myra Hydley. The image he
recreated had been so repeatedly used in
the British press that it is deeply imprinted in
the minds of the UK public. When displayed
at the Sensation exhibition in 1997 the
painting was attacked, the gallery was
picketed, windows were smashed and the

painting removed before being re-hung
behind protective Perspex, guarded by
security men. *The Times* newspaper's art
critic wrote that: 'Far from cynically exploiting
her notoriety, Harvey's grave and monumental
canvas succeeds in conveying the enormity
of the crime she committed. Seen from afar,
through several doorways, Hindley's face
looms at us like an apparition. By the time
we get close enough to realise that it is
spattered with children's handprints, the
sense of menace becomes overwhelming.'
See Rescaling.

Image building

The Italian artist Giuseppe Arcimboldo created famous paintings of heads that consisted of images of flowers, fruit and vegetables. During the wars between England and France at the beginning of the nineteenth century the faces of the Duke of Wellington and Napoleon were re-created by caricaturists on both sides. The leaders were seen as heroic when their faces were constructed from patriotic images and despotic when they were built from the tools of death and the dead. *See* Caricature, Making faces.

Collective power

When David Gentleman was commissioned to design placards for demonstrators who attended the 2003 march against war with Iraq, he created a message in huge type that simply said NO. A million people took part in the protest. War artist John Keane wrote that when all the placards were seen together they 'created a forest of "No's" filling the London streets, making one unchallengeable statement.'

Johann Michael Voltz, *Napoleon*, 1813
German artist Voltz viciously attacked Napoleon in this caricature printed during the Franco-Prussian War. It is said to have sold 20,000 copies in a week. It is an amazing multi-faceted piece of anti-Napoleon propaganda: his face is made from the bodies of those killed by his warmongering, their nakedness symbolizing their innocence. The anxious-looking eagle represents France as a worried nation, while the uniform is composed of a map of Germany depicting the battles of the war. The emperor's epaulette is a hand made up of all the forces united against him, which unravels a spider's web, symbolizing the flimsy gains of the French forces. *See* Making maps, Symbols.

DIY
Find a relationship between two or more elements in your project or brief. Build an image that reveals one element and use the others as building blocks.

Brainjack
Images built from smaller elements create a sense of wonder and admiration in a viewer. The greater the number of pieces used to make a picture, the greater the awe. There is tension between the pieces and the final image they create, in particular if there is a jarring or revealing relationship between the two. An example is the giant image of the child murderer Myra Hindley (*see* previous page).

Caricature

Caricature visually accentuates and mocks the faults of the powerful, corrupt, pompous and vain. It mercilessly ridicules and pillories politicians, royalty and the famous. Jonathan Swift, author of Gulliver's Travels, *advised that politicians should be repeatedly pinched, pricked and punched to remind them of their forgotten promises; caricatures miss no opportunity to attack targets by transforming them into bloated pigs, preening peacocks, incontinent drunkards and ravenous cannibals.*

James Gillray, *An excrescence – a fungus; alias a toadstool upon a dunghill,* **1791** Master satiricist Gillray's caricatures lacerate the pretensions of the powerful – here he turns the head of Prime Minister William Pitt into that of a diseased toadstool with the blotchy swollen features of a drunk. Its roots engulf the crown – which represents the monarchy – mired in excrement. *See* One thing looks like another.

'*Caricature is always Us against Them. The joke is shared; so is the hate.*'
William Feaver, writer

'*The underdogs get to laugh at those who think they're the top dogs.*'
John Baxter, artist

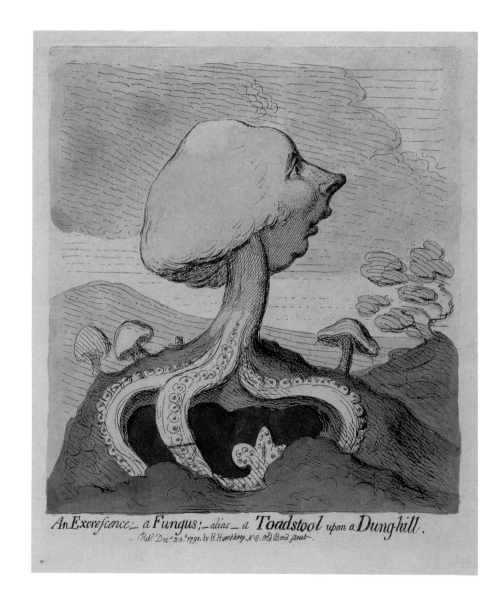

An Excrefcence;— a Fungus;—*alias— a* **Toadstool** *upon a* **Dunghill**.
— *Pubᵈ Decʳ 20.ᵗʰ 1791. by H. Humphrey Nº 8. Old Bond ſtreet* —

A master satirist
Some brilliant unpublished drawings by James Gillray recently came to light. They date from a golden age of caricature at the beginning of the nineteenth century, and ridiculed the king and politicians with such venom and offensiveness that Gillray's publisher felt he had to suppress them in order to avoid prison.

Fluck and Law, *Thatcha!*, 1989
Peter Fluck and Roger Law are the 20th century's Gillray and Hogarth. They pilloried royalty and politicians throughout the 1980s and 90s with their outrageous weekly UK TV show *Spitting Image*. Two hundred years after Gillray attacked William Pitt (see previous page) they target another Prime Minister, this time Margaret Thatcher who demonically slices Britain from the rest of the world. At its height, a quarter of England's adult population watched the programme. *See* Making maps.

 DIY
Amplify and exaggerate the significant characteristics of your target while diminishing the factors you feel are insignificant. Learn from the searing and wonderful caricatures of William Hogarth, James Gillray, George Cruikshank, Johann Michael Voltz, Honoré Daumier, Charles Philipon (*see* One thing looks like another), J. J. Grandville (*see* Shadows), John Tenniel, A. A. Gaillard, Edward Linley Sambourne, Jean Veber, George Grosz, H. M. Bateman, David Low, Ralph Steadman and Gerald Scarfe (*see* Satire).

 Brainjack
Caricatures reveal and massively enlarge what we suspect or know to be true. Viewers feel they are in agreement, and collusion, with the caricaturist. The more shocking or daring the revelation, the greater the impact.

Clichés seen afresh

A visual cliché is an image we have grown tired of; it used to work just fine but has become stale and devalued through overuse. A cliché can be resuscitated and jolted back into life by a fresh and imaginative reinvention.

Jonathan Barnbrook, *The Evolution of Man*, 2004 (above)
In the 50 years since it first appeared the illustration 'The March of Progress' by Rudolph Zallinger showing the evolution of man has become overused and clichéd. In this design, one of a series of anti-war images created for a billboard artvertising project shown in a Paris park, multidisciplinary designer Barnbrook revitalizes the image by turning the final figure back on the others, thus reversing expectations. *See* www.barnbrook.net

Ben Cannon, Viewfinder Film Festival poster, 2006 (right)
Images of clapperboards, film cans, projector spools, sprocketed cine film, directors' chairs and cine cameras are the clichés of film festival promotion. Here photographer Ben Cannon's wonderfully energetic and simple use of sparklers and a bunch of his friends to roughly draw a camera and type create a modern and exciting poster for this cult UK film festival – breathing fresh life into the camera as a symbol for creative film making. *See* Symbols, www.bencannon.co.uk

 DIY
Embrace clichés, then rejuvenate them. Assemble all the visual ones associated with your brief then look at ways of reusing them, and reconnecting to their essence with new vigour.

 Brainjack
A cliché seen afresh has twice its original potency. A viewer can both get the message and recognize the smartness of the reinvention. It's double-strength communication.

Colour

Jannuzzi Smith, Colours of Scotland, postage stamps, 2001
Multidisciplinary design group Jannuzzi Smith created this series of stamps for the Royal Mail inspired by the colours of Scotland. Photographs by David Rowland, Arnhel de Serra and Fleur Olby. *See www.jannuzzismith.com*

Jamie Dobson, Record colour order, 2005 (opposite below)
Designer and photographer Dobson was inspired to rearrange his entire record album collection in colours rather than the usual musical genres. The resulting reshuffle of the wafer-thin spines creates a harmonious installation. *See www.jamiedobson.com*

Colour is inspiring. The fashion designer Paul Smith created an entire collection after seeing a security guard at a palace in Beijing wearing a uniform of the deepest blue; and one of the most successful fabrics he produced was based on the vivid colours of the traditional dress of Guatemala.

The natural world is also a source of inspiration. For example, the Highlands, hillsides, rocks and sea of Scotland inspire the colours of traditional weaves of tartans and tweeds. In the man-made world every city and town has its unique palette made up from its buildings, streets, stores, food, produce and local dress, together with the harshness or softness of the sunlight in its geographic location. The colours of Bologna in northern Italy, for example, are those of mustards – from bright yellow English mustard to the darker Dijon variety.

'One of the great masters [of colour] was Matisse. He often put colours together that normally aren't seen together, which can create striking moods – cool, minimal, eccentric.'
Paul Smith, fashion designer

'I like colour that is impressionistic and mysterious rather than real. I admire the swilling, blurred action pictures of Ernst Haas and the soft, grainy colour of Sarah Moon. Pure reality recorded in colour seems to me like a data book – true, but uninspiring.'
Tony Jones, photographer

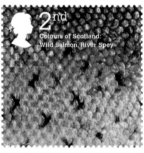

The colours of things
Gold, silver, bronze, terracotta, brick, lemon, orange, blood-orange, plum, cherry, raspberry, lobster, olive, camel, burgundy, chestnut, camel, battleship grey, Guantanamo orange, pillarbox red, chocolate brown, charcoal grey, forest green, sludge brown, chalk white, strawberry blonde, pea green, sky blue, blood red.

Be inspired by the colours of the past
Every era has its own colours: in the 1960s they were predominantly bright, hot, primary and crisp, while the 1980s was a time of black and chrome, when domestic interiors looked like sterile offices.

Be inspired by colour in photography
Creative photographers use colour in exciting ways: Guy Bourdin, Sarah Moon, David LaChapelle and Wolfgang Tillmans all use very different colour palettes in their work.

Be inspired by colour in art and the movies
Seek inspiration from the memorable use of colour in art and the movies. The English cinematographer Jack Cardiff said he gained his mastery of colour and light by spending hours looking at paintings in the National Gallery in London. His partnership with the film directors Michael Powell and Emeric Pressburger produced movies of sumptuous colour, such as *A Matter of Life and Death, Black Narcissus* and *The Red Shoes*. Later in his career Cardiff directed movies including *Girl on a Motorcyle* which, though poorly scripted, featured throbbing, near-hallucinogenic colour. *See* Art, Movies.

Creative colours
A great example of the creative use of colour in recent movies is director Steven Soderbergh's *Traffic* in which each of the interweaving stories is defined by a different use of colour; one features bleached-out yellows, another deep blues. Another example is *The Godfather* with its use of orange.

A spectrum of colour
Colours can be: Technicolor, clashing, muted, sombre, candyfloss, psychedelic, toxic, exotic, neon, insipid, vivid, organic, natural, unnatural, artificial, primary, complementary, uncomplementary, hot, cold, intense, oppressive, sumptuous.

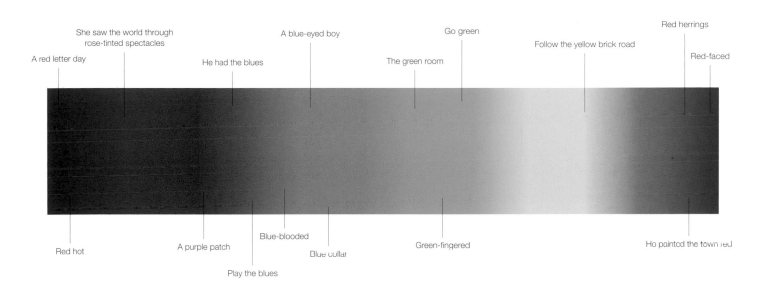

She saw the world through rose-tinted spectacles · A blue-eyed boy · Go green · Red herrings · A red letter day · He had the blues · The green room · Follow the yellow brick road · Red-faced

Red hot · A purple patch · Blue-blooded · Green-fingered · He painted the town red · Play the blues · Blue collar

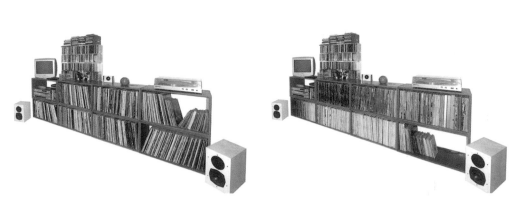

DIY
Choose colours for communication with care. Consider the emotion you wish to provoke. Collect colours – both clashing ones and those that harmonize. Examine attempts that have been made to give values to colour by grouping ones that jar or complement. Be inspired by the colours of the natural and man-made worlds.

Brainjack
Colours can communicate to a viewer's emotions and provoke strong feelings. Combinations of colours that clash or harmonize can also grab the attention.

Counter-
intuition

The world looks flat – but, hey, what if it's the opposite?
To counter something is to take the opposite viewpoint.
A counter-intuitive idea is one that takes the current
and conventional wisdom and turns it on its head.

Paul Smith menswear catalogue, 1993
The casting of people with lined and lived-
in faces – rather than professional models
considered the peak of human beauty –
counters a century of fashion photography.
Art direction by Alan Aboud, photography
by David Bailey.

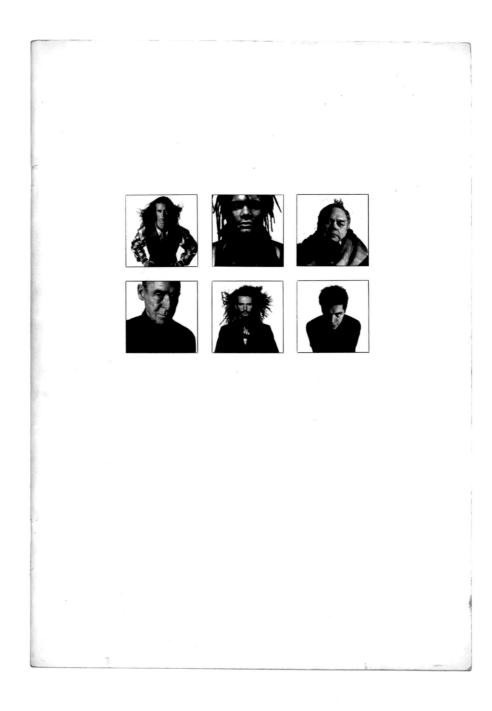

Rethink everything you think is true

In the long history of vacuum-cleaning every manufacturer designed their machines to gather the dust in disposable bags. It was thought that dust was unsightly and no one would want to see it. This was until James Dyson rethought what was thought to be true. He took the totally opposite view and created machines that showed what had been sucked up. His hugely popular vacuum clearers give users a sense of both cleanliness and achievement as they can see all the dust they are getting rid of.

Tide-turning counter-intuition

While all Apple's competitors produced home computers that looked like drab grey boxes, the company's chief designer, Jonathan Ive, created revolutionary see-through coloured monitors that showed the machine's innards. The massive sales that followed turned the tide for Apple: for the first time a computer was seen as an object that could be both aesthetically beautiful and complementary to the interiors of modern homes.

Counter-intuitive casting

The convention in advertising and fashion imagery is that the people featured should be young, skinny, tall and beautiful with perfect hair, skin and teeth in order to fit what are thought to be the aspirations of consumers. Defying these conventions can create striking and memorable results, as can be seen in fashion photography's use of 'street casting' of normal people of all ages instead of using conventional models.

Droog, Heat Wave, radiator, 2006 (above)
Radiators have always been ugly things, boxed off and hidden away until designer Joris Laarman created the wonderfully ornate Heat Wave for pioneering Dutch design group Droog. Its beautifully decorative wave form demands to be shown off rather than hidden. The decoration is also functional as the increased surface area radiates more heat than conventional designs. *Droog* is the Dutch word for 'dry' or 'wry' – echoing their design manifesto that 'no nonsense meets humour'. *See* Fusion, www.droog.com

DIY
Be contrary. Dismantle what you are asked to do. Look at the conventions and explore the opposites (*see* Reversing problems). Always question the status quo. Play against conventions. Always ask why things are as they are, and why do they have to stay that way?

Brainjack
A counter-intuitive idea can be exciting and revelatory to viewers as everything they thought was true has been overturned.

Creative collisions

There are numerous commonly used visual languages with which viewers feel cosy and comfortable. Even glimpsed from afar, their style immediately communicates what they are about to tell you. As soon as they are seen their message is anticipated.

Such conventions of image and type can be excitingly exploited by using them in creative collisions in which the way visual style and message are combined totally defies expectations.

Exhibition poster, 1985 (right)
The visual language of the boxing prize-fight poster is reused for this memorable advert for a show of paintings by Andy Warhol and Jean-Michel Basquiat. Warhol is the old champ and Basquiat the young contender in this creative collision.

Paul Smith mainline brochure, 1994 (opposite)
Art director Alan Aboud reused the vivid Technicolor palette, crinkle cut-edges and simple typography unique to the much-loved John Hinde brand of holiday postcards to create a quintessentially British catalogue for quintessentially British designer Paul Smith. Speaking about this campaign Aboud recalls – 'we had an eccentric client and we wanted to create eccentric images. There had just been a very small exhibition of the John Hinde postcard images, for me it was my childhood, images I'd grown up with. He shot all of these images in his front porch and put them together – he was like a human Photoshop. For the postcards campaign there was no market research, no focus group, we just grabbed the clothes, picked the models and away we went. We didn't use professional models just friends. You get excitement if you do it differently. There's a big adrenaline rush.' *See* You! (put yourself in it).

Politics, satire, music
The political paintings of Bob and Roberta Smith use the visual language of corner-shop lettering, while Alison Jackson's satirical photographs are created to look like grabbed paparazzi pictures. The Ukulele Orchestra of Great Britain plays grunge music.

Spectacular collisions

The styles of trade union banners, aeroplane safety cards, embroidered samplers, loveheart sweets, gravestones, pizza boxes and memorial plaques are familiar, and their customary mixtures of image, text and materials have been excitingly subverted in memorable creative collisions.

Likewise, the visual language of boxing posters, fairground and circus posters, newspaper billboards, pin-ups, courtroom drawings, saucy seaside postcards, church posters and lost pet posters has been used to communicate unanticipated messages.

DIY
Collect visual languages and use them in unexpected ways. Remix them. The greater the collision, the bigger the crash, and the more engaging the result.

Brainjack
The unexpected use of visual language can create a 'crash' in viewers' minds as the language and how it has been used collide. It can both attract their attention and delight them, by confounding expectations of how things are meant to be done, engaging them to ask: 'What on earth is going on here?'

A photo opportunity at Big Ben

Relaxing after a night in Swinging London

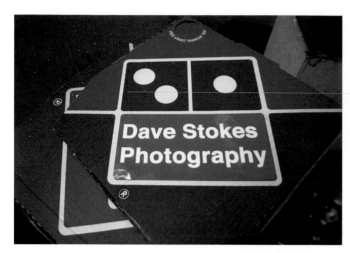

Dave Stokes, Pizza box portfolio, 2009 (far left)
Photographer Dave Stokes surprised visitors at a student exhibition with his portfolio when they were expecting a Domino's pizza.

Pizza delivery (left top)
A pizza box delivers a message for punk band The Clash.

Cool brand (left middle)
T-shirt packaging and display from the Chinese brand Shirtflag.

Nicole Davies and Leah Evans, Lovehearts, 2009 (below and left below)
Usually featuring teasing messages to be exchanged flirtatiously, here loveheart sweets are recreated for a powerful sexual heath awareness campaign.

Why Not Associates, Exhibition poster, 2000 (bottom)
A cosy 'stock' image of a couple frolicking in the sea clashingly collides with the theme of this exhibition of contemporary art.
See www.whynotassociates.com

Yang Yongliang, *Phantom Landscape no.2*, 2006 (above)
From a distance this work by Shanghai-born Yang Yongliang appears to be a beautiful brush-painted landscape created in a highly traditional style. In close-up it becomes clear the image is made of up thousands of photographs collaged together using advanced digital techniques. Scenes of modern-day flyovers, massive cranes and construction sites fuse to create an image in which ancient and contemporary visions of China crash together. *See* Illusion.

Hot Deals Baghdad, poster, 2003 (left)
In Feburary 2003 students at St Martins College of Art in London were briefed to make work reflecting on the looming war against Iraq. This poster hijacks the visual language of the contemporary campaign for Easyjet.

Fabrica, 2398 gr, book packaging, 2003 (above)
Instead of chicken korma or special fried rice this takeaway carton contains a book exploring our relationships with food.

Cryptic communication

The use of codes for communication is known as cryptology. A code is a system of letters, numbers or symbols into which language can be converted to allow information to be communicated in secrecy. the everyday use of cryptology is seen in cryptic crosswords in newspapers. The one in The Times *is so popular that for many years it was the only aspect of any newspaper in the United Kingdom that readers would pay for online.*

Neville Brody, *I Hate Design* rebus, magazine cover, 2009 (above)
Brody created this attention-grabbing rebus message to readers when guest designer at ultra-trendy design mag *Wallpaper**.

Trickett and Webb, *Ideas* rebus, 1991 (right)
This cryptic message created for a self-promotional brochure by London-based design group Trickett and Webb imaginatively conveys to potential clients that they're great at ideas and communication.

Cryptic clues

A cryptic clue is a phrase or sentence that seems to make sense. It leads the reader in one direction, putting ideas in their head – but this is often a diversion or false trail. The answer is derived by interpreting the clue in less obvious ways. To solve it the reader has to get on the same brain wavelength as the person who created it. Part of the joy of a crossword is understanding how the creator's brain works.

People have their favourite cluemasters, credited at the side of the crosswords they make – cryptically, of course.

Inspect a rebus

Rebus means 'by things' in Latin, and is a cryptic visual message in which some words or letters are represented by things. Milton Glaser's 'I ❤ NY' is the most famous rebus of all time.

Rebuses are incredibly playful and imaginative ways of communicating and offer many different levels of complexity. One art student had a poster on his wall for months before he suddenly noticed it was more than a beautiful design; it was also a rebus.

Start making finance less puzzling

WE LIVE IN
FT
FINANCIAL TIMES

Find your free student subscription to FT.com via facebook.

(A) Real time updates.

Start making finance less puzzling

WE LIVE IN
FT
FINANCIAL TIMES

Find your free student subscription to FT.com via Facebook.

(A) Time your archive.

Tom Ford, *Financial Times* **ads, 2010**
Advertising student Tom Ford challenges readers to solve these cryptic ads.

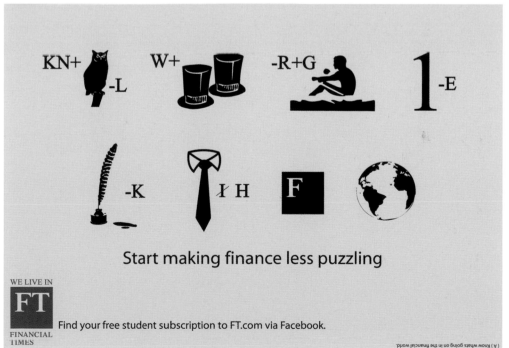

Start making finance less puzzling

WE LIVE IN
FT
FINANCIAL TIMES

Find your free student subscription to FT.com via Facebook.

(A) Know whats going on in the financial world.

DIY
Collect and study cryptic communication. Challenge your viewers to solve the clues. Ensure the clues are on the right wavelength for your audience.

Brainjack
Cryptic messages tease the brain and engage people by challenging them to solve clues and complete a puzzle. They are a very interactive form of communication, as the viewer has to really work at it. They are also delayed-action communication, as the viewer has to strive to get the message. Reward and gratification come from successfully solving the conundrum by decoding the message and recognizing false trails and deceptions within the clues.

Digitality

Our early evolution has been recorded through the principal materials we used creatively – we moved from the Stone Age through the Iron Age into the Bronze Age. Today we have reached the Digital Age. Digital technologies provide a rapidly developing stream of inspiration for creative people. Digitality offers the opportunity to fuse ideas with computer technology, electronics, sensors, sound, music, cameras, screens, projectors, lights, lasers, machines and new venues for messages.

Moving Brands, The Looking Glass, digital exhibition, 2008 (top)
Briefed to showcase the work of 600 students graduating from 40 different courses at the London College of Fashion design group Moving Brands created a picture postcard for each student which when placed on a series of custom-built responsive tables triggered interactive projections of the respective student's creative work. *See* www.movingbrands.com

Design Act, Pixel Cloud Skyscraper, digital building, 2009 (above)
A design for the Singapore pavilion at the World Expo takes the form of a massive cloud of digital screens.

Hussein Chalayan, digital dress, 2007 (right)
Cypriot-born fashion designer Hussein Chalayan makes highly innovate use of materials and technology in his clothes. This digital dress features tens of thousands of LEDs embedded in the fabric that can be programmed to ripple, pulse and display images.

Mehmet Akten, Body Paint, digital installation (opposite)
Akten's interactive installation has been described as a 'visual instrument' on which visitors can compose their own paintings.

Digital conversations

The most exciting creative digital work features elements in which the responses and behaviour of the audience trigger live interaction. Digitality can go beyond simply sending a message as it offers the opportunity to instigate a conversation between a creator and a viewer.

Digital painting

Turkish-born designer Mehmet Akten created the large-scale interactive installation *Body Paint* (*see* below), in which the movements and gestures of people standing in front of it create splashes, blurs and waves of vibrant colour that change in reaction to the speed and boldness with which the viewers move.

Breathtaking digitality

Some artists and designers have created incredibly subtle and sensitive digital work; for example, the digital dresses designed by Hussein Chalayan (*see* opposite), are spellbinding. A recent exhibition of pioneering creative digitality at the Victoria & Albert Museum in London featured a strangely beautiful, projected silhouette of a large, gently swaying tree in the darkened gallery, its movements activated by the breeze in the street outside. Occasionally, projected leaves fell gently to the floor. *See* Museums, Silhouettes.

Digital architecture

The Singapore-based design group Design Act proposed an amazing digital building for their entry to a competition to create Singapore's pavilion for the Shanghai 2010 Expo (*see* opposite). The building, nicknamed the Pixel Cloud Skyscraper, featured 3,866 digital cubes of varying sizes on to which visitors, beckoned inside by music, could post their dreams of tomorrow. The plan was to create a hovering, ever-changing digital cloud.

The British designer Thomas Heatherwick created the British pavilion for the expo. Made of 60,000 fibre-optic rods that appear to burst from the building's core, at night it pulsed with colours in response to the wind.

OMG, a digital chandelier

Challenged to create a chandelier that merged technology and innovation with tradition, Israeli-born designer Ron Arad designed a twisting corkscrew shape made of over 2,000 crystals and 1,000 white LEDs (*see* overleaf). The chandelier is designed to receive and display text messages, which pulse slowly downwards around its curves. *See* Unexpected venues.

Domestic digital art

French artist Thomas Charvériat concealed mini tape players that could be triggered remotely using the internet inside refrigerators and washing machines; each one featured brief snatches of speech. He sold the machines on eBay and, in the following months, occasionally set off the tape players so that householders suddenly found their white goods talking to them. A little shamefaced about this invasion of other people's privacy, he decided to let strangers invade his own home and linked the lighting, television, music system and switches to all the domestic appliances in his apartment to a website which enabled anyone who logged on anywhere in the world to turn them on and off at will. Cameras relayed the action live on the website.

Domestic digital design

Robin Southgate designed a toaster that forewarns breakfasters about the day's weather. It is linked to meteorological forecasts on the internet which trigger the appliance to imprint symbols for sunny, cloudy or rainy on the surface of the toast.

'The moment that really turned me on to working digitally was seeing an exhibition at the Royal College of Art in London of what was then called computer-related design. There were all these strange experiments including one with a golden curtain, sized about 3 by 1.8 metres (10 x 6ft), made of thousands of large sequins. When you walked past it billowed and followed you while playing a burst of music. When you walked back again it billowed and followed you again. People were just transfixed by it; they just stopped and started interacting with it. It was totally engaging and highly immediate. Later I discovered it was incredibly simple, with a video camera and a series of fans. The video camera saw where you were and just blew the fans. Like all the best digital work the technology was invisible; you simply engaged with the idea.'

Ross Cooper, multidisciplinary designer

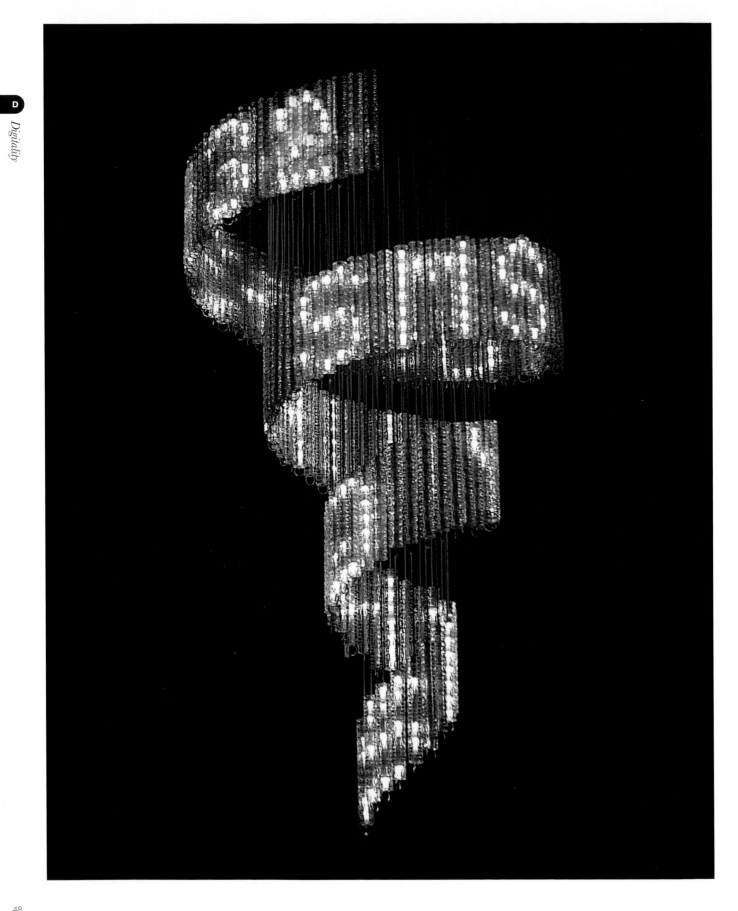

Digital light sculpture

The artist Phillip Vaughan pioneered the interaction between the elements and creativity in his light sculpture Hayward Neon Tower *installed on London's South Bank in 1972 with electronics engineered by Roger Dainton. It featured dozens of neon tubes that turned on and off in response to the speed with which a small meteorological windmill within the structure rotated.*

DIY
We are at the dawn of digitality; explore and experiment with current digital technology to the maximum. Find new connections between technologies. Embrace digitality and its possibilities. Use its gifts. The technology provides huge opportunities for designers to create original ways to communicate and converse with an audience.

Ensure that the technology involved is always invisible, so that viewers are solely engaged with the ideas.

Brainjack
Creative people have always striven to engage and involve their audience in their work. Digital technology enables viewers to participate physically in a piece of design or art – which can be a captivating experience.

Digitality can be immersive, and demand the viewer's time and concentration.

Heatherwick Studios, UK Pavillion, Expo, China, digital building, 2010 (below)
Thomas Heatherwick's stunning building pulses in the dark responding to the breeze. Photos by Geoff Putnam.

Ron Arad, Lolita chandelier, 2004 (opposite)
Arad's reinvention of the chandelier for the late 20th century, it can receive and display text messages. *See* Reinvention.

Thomas Charvériat, Lui Dao, Zane Mellupe, Chen Xin, Yang Longhai, Yan Jiaping, Rose Tang, Impulse Momentum 01, digital artwork, 2009 (above)
The observer becomes participant as lights and audio speakers respond to the movements of the audience triggered by sensors woven into the undulating surface of this digital artwork. *See* www.Island6.org

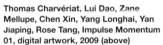

The age of digitality (above and left)
Digital buildings, projections, advertisements and screens are now ubiquitious in every major city.

Dreams and daydreams

'The best things I've done, I've done from dreams.'
Karl Lagerfeld, fashion designer

'I can dream all day long and ideas for paintings just fall into my mind like slides.'
Francis Bacon, painter

'I try to make work that looks like my dreams.'
Charlie Kaufman, film director and screenwriter of the *Eternal Sunshine of the Spotless Mind* and *Being John Malkovich*

'If you can dream it – you can do it.'
Walt Disney, animator and film producer

'What we need is men to dream of the impossible.'
John F. Kennedy

'I am a professional dreamer.'
Philippe Starck, designer

'If you couldn't play rock 'n' roll what would you do?'
'I'd be a full-time dreamer.'
Marty DiBergi (question) and David St Hubbins (answer) in *This Is Spinal Tap*

'The inspiration for our collection comes from surrealism, from the work of Jean Cocteau, Salvador Dalí and Man Ray.'
Designers Domenico Dolce and Stefano Gabbana, interviewed in *Vogue* magazine

Great ideas can come from the unconscious world of dreams – we dream them up. During sleep our brains go out to play, escaping from the constraints of our waking hours. In dreams we think in a different way.

Dreams are visual and can create extraordinarily distinctive visions that rearrange, amplify, distort, condense and combine things in fantastic new ways. Dreams link to desires and inner hopes.

Daydreaming is the pleasurable, transient state between consciousness and sleep when thoughts and images appear in the mind. This, too, is a highly creative time.

'It's so surreal'

The artists of the Surrealist movement put dreams and the forces of the unconscious mind at the centre of their creativity. Nearly a hundred years after its birth Surrealism continues to be the most inspirational of art movements. It has inspired amazing work by graphic designers, advertising creatives, photographers, illustrators, film- and video-makers, fashion designers, interior and product designers, comedians and performers as well as generations of artists. Surrealist artists attempted to use periods of self-induced sleep deprivation as a catalyst for generating ideas.

Unfortunately, the word surreal has been watered down and is now often used to describe anything that is in the least bit odd or unexpected.

'You have about ten minutes to act on an idea before it recedes back to dreamland.'
Buckminster Fuller, designer

'I often get ideas quite late at night, just before sleep. I have to turn the light on, write it down or sketch it. Having got it down on paper I can then sleep.'
Ross Cooper, multidisciplinary designer.

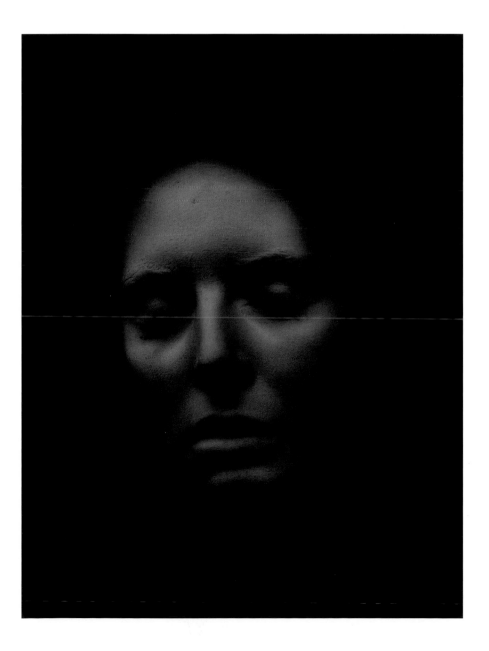

Joanna Kane, *The Somnambulists*, 2008
Kane created a stunning series of photographs of the plaster life casts and death masks kept in the collections of the Scottish National Portrait Gallery and the Phrenological Society of Edinburgh. The pictures were published in her book *The Somnambulists* – a word for sleepwalkers – where the faces appear in a dreamlike trance between life, death and sleep. The photograph of the male face (opposite) is of poet Samuel Taylor Coleridge, the female face (this page) is of an unknown woman. *See* www.joannakane.co.uk.

 DIY
Follow your dreams. Most people spend about two decades asleep during their lives. Ensure this time is maximized by embracing dreams and daydreams as a creative force. Record ideas swiftly before they drift away. Study the work and potency of Surrealist art and design.

Imagine your waking life is a dream and your dreams are real life!

 Brainjack
Dreams and daydreams derail usual trains of thought. They offer radically different ways of thinking to conscious thoughts and can therefore produce compellingly different visions.

E

Expressions visualized

Everyday language is dense with expressions that can be recreated visually: He minced his words. They were a puppet government. He went off the rails. Life is a bowl of cherries. Life is a bed of roses. He's lost his marbles. It puts hair on your chest. He's a moneybags. Money doesn't grown on trees. He was stabbed in the back. She put her foot in her mouth. They had blood on their hands. It was a bloodbath. He threw in the towel. He threw his toys out of the pram. He was spineless. It cost an arm and a leg. They'll have the shirt off your back. She was clutching at straws. It was the last straw. They're on the gravy train. She was skating on thin ice. Too big for his boots. Put yourself in his shoes. Take a backhander. He was rooted to the spot.

Miles Calcraft Briginshaw Duffy,
***Hooked*, anti-smoking ad, 2007 (right)**
This ad created for the UK Department of Heath so shocked the British public that it was banned by advertising watchdogs.

***Off the Rail*, cartoon from *Punch*, 1849 (opposite)**
Railway financier George Hudson goes off the rails. Known as 'the railway king' he was ruined following the disclosure of fraud and the bribery of Members of Parliament.

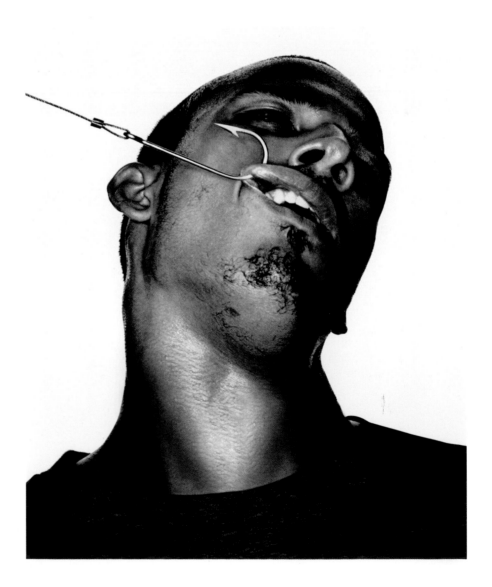

OFF THE RAIL.

The Plumb-pudding in danger : — or — State Epicures taking un Petit Souper.
— "the great Globe itself, and all which it inherit", is too small to satisfy such insatiable appetites.

SAY NO TO NO SAY.

Using alcohol as a crutch (opposite)
Illustration for a newspaper feature on alcoholism.

James Gillray, *The Plumb-Pudding in Danger*, 1805 (top)
British prime minister William Pitt and the French emperor Napoleon carve up the world between them – cutting off more than they can chew.

Boase Massimi Pollitt Univas partnership, *Red Tape*, 1984 (above)
This ad protests at the proposed closure by the British Government of the Greater London Council in 1986 – the GLC was the elected body responsible for administering the British capital. The ad's creators pioneered the inventive use of advertising billboard spaces by wrapping selected posters in red tape – representing stifling bureaucracy – causing huge publicity and awareness of the campaign.

 DIY
Collect visual phrases. Examine language and words that relate to your work and could be expressed in imagery. *See* Wordplay.

Examine visual phrases in other languages. For example, a regular customer at a café in France is said to 'have a pillow on the bar'. In Australia someone who easily becomes drunk is known as a 'two-pot screamer'. In China an eccentric person is said to be 'thirteen o'clock'. In Colombia 'Chinese whispers' – where a message becomes increasingly distorted through repetition – is known as 'broken telephone'; the Chinese do not seem to have an equivalent expression.

 Brainjack
Viewers are engaged when they recognize an expression and its translation from the verbal to the visual.

Eyes

You can solve any brief with an image of an eye. Eyes are both compelling and visually dynamic; a stare can be powerfully hypnotic. Their flexibility in design can be seen in the fact that they have been used to represent both creative individuality in posters for art and design exhibitions, and to portray the terror of Big Brother's all-seeing totalitarian regime in covers for George Orwell's 1984.

Visual Communication, book jacket, 2008 (right)
A word balloon – a symbol for communication – becomes the white of an eye in this cover that simply and elegantly expresses the title. Design by Jon Allan. *See* Symbols.

Crystallize, Swarovski ad, 2007 (far right)
This 2007 campaign for Swarovski Elements, the premium brand for the finest crystal elements was shot by British photographer Nick Knight. His highly innovative fashion and advertising work is showcased on his website www.showstudio.com.

Electric shock for the eyes, 1995 (below)
Announcing the French Art Directors awards ceremony, this poster wonderfully evokes their aim – to jolt the eyes of consumers into life with their work. Produced by agency TBWA, the photography is by Dimitri Daniloff.

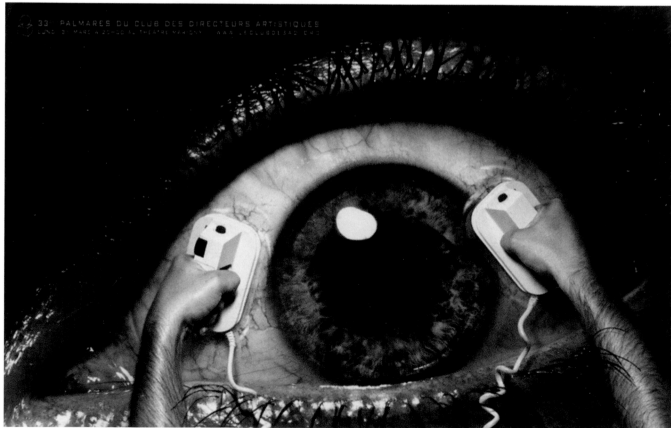

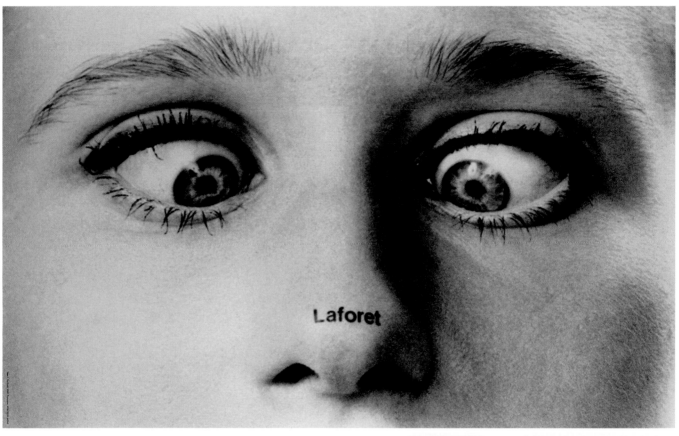

Eye, eye (above)
Advertisement designed by Art Director
Takuya Onuki for Tokyo's hip department
store Laforet who commission leading
artists and designers to create striking
and witty imagery.

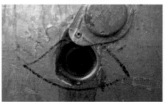

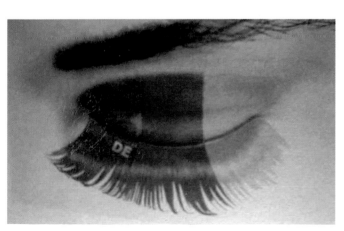

German eye, 1998 (above)
An image of an eye used to encapsulate
an entire nation. Design group Wolff Olins
created this chic image in a project that
aimed to celebrate the modernity and
forward-looking ambitions of a newly
unified Germany.

Seeing eyes (above)
Eyes found in the street and in the park.
The painted eye is a symbol painted on
the windows of vacant shops in cities in
China, it indicates to potential burglars
that the owners are vigilantly keeping
an eye on their property.

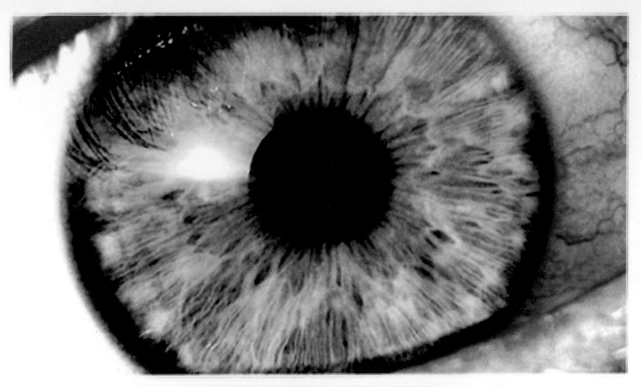

UNIVERSITY OF GLOUCESTERSHIRE
UNLEASHED
EDITORIAL AND ADVERTISING PHOTOGRAPHY 2007

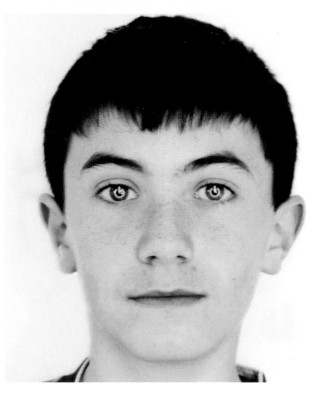

Call for entries

Images 34
The best of British contemporary illustration 2010

Deadline: Friday 31st July 2009

Illustration 'CCTV Loud-Hailer' by Frazer Hudson

Oi!

To enter go to www.aoiimages.com

AOI ▶ **Association of illustrators**

**Kieran Hunt, *Unleashed*, poster, 2007
(opposite top)**
Hunt created this beautiful photograph for
a poster that announced an exhibition by
graduating photography students – using the
eye as a symbol of creativity and individuality.
See Symbols, www.Kieranhunt.com.

Eye-opener (opposite bottom left)
Graphic artist Jimmy Turrell created this
eye-opening piece about evolution.
See www.jimmyturrell.com

**Samantha Bourne and Kelly Morse,
Disconnected from Reality, poster,
2010 (opposite bottom right)**
A poster promoting a science festival talk
about the isolating effects of the internet on
young people.

Eye-catching (above)
Frazer Hudson created this eye-catching
announcement for the UK Association of
Illustrators. *See* www.fraserhudson.com.

DIY
Make eye contact: when you
receive a brief seek connections
to vision and eyes.

Brainjack
The eyes have it. Their expressive
ability can convey the whole
spectrum of emotions from joy
to terror. Images of eyes deliver
instant messages: a black eye
= violence, bloodshot eyes =
tiredness or a hangover, tears
in the eyes = sadness, eyes
propped open with matchsticks
= exhaustion, a wink = a friendly
greeting or shared joke.

F

Familiar but seen afresh

Connecting new ideas to established formats and long-running campaigns can immediately grab the viewer's attention. Piggybacking on the deeply familiar can be a short cut to quick communication.

Copper Greene, *iRaq*, 2004
The iPod silhouette campaign is brilliantly usurped in this 2004 flyposter pasted around New York protesting against the horrific torture of prisoners in Abu Ghraib military prison and the occupation of Iraq. It was created by the collective Copper Greene using the picture of the hooded prisoner undergoing torture that has been described as 'an image of evil' and 'the most haunting image of the early twenty-first century'. Copper Greene took their name from the code name for the secret US black ops programme that allegedly encouraged the highly illegal physical abuse and sexual humiliation techniques used on the prisoners of war. *iRaq* provoked the young iPod generation – generally unbothered by politics – into debate about the war. *See* Photographs.

Artverts and subverts

In addition to adding extra elements to formats that are already imprinted on viewers' minds, overpasting and overpainting sections of familiar advertisements has been used successfully to subvert messages. In Australia B.U.G.A. U.P. (Billboard Utilizing Graffitists Against Unhealthy Promotions), a group of phantom graffiti sprayers, oversprayed an iconic Marlboro cowboy cigarette advertisement which originally read New. Mild and Marlboro to deliver the anti-smoking message New. Vile a Bore.

⊖ beware pickpockets

Cut iPod, London Transport ad (above)
The highly familiar visual language of the iPod campaign is here smartly reused for a London Transport anti-pick-pocketing campaign.

The Bee Books (left)
The cosy style of illustration, cover design and format of the much-loved Ladybird books is reemployed for these health and sex education publications for young adults.

DIY
Examine an established visual communication that is familiar to your audience, then use its visual aesthetic to deliver your message.

Brainjack
The viewer expects the next in a long line of similar messages but instead finds something surpricingly different.

Finding ideas

Inspiration is all around us. You can be inspired on your doorstep, at work and in the street. There are things you come across in everyday life that you couldn't make up: unexpected coincidences, joyous juxtapositions and accidental visual poetry. Magnificence can be stumbled across in the mundane. Take inspiration from chance observations and discoveries.

'Always keep your eyes open. Never go to sleep in the car. Whatever you see can inspire you.'
Grace Coddington, fashion editor

Andy Freeberg, *Sentry***, 2006**
American photographer Freeberg found the idea for this series of photos after witnessing the behaviour of gallery staff to their visitors at the numerous private art galleries in Manhattan. He followed the series by photographing the ladies who are the guardians of the artwork in Russian museums. *See* www.andyfreeberg.com

Finding ideas underneath you

In the early 1920s the designer Marcel Breuer was inspired while he was cycling on his new bicycle. It was tubular, sleek and strong, and he thought: 'I could design other things using this material.' His Breuer chair is still in production nearly a hundred years later. Similarly, the inspiration for the Anglepoise lamp came from the springed suspension under cars.

'Leonardo advised young painters to look at damp-stained walls and unevenly coloured stones in order to stimulate their imagination.'

Anthony Storr, *The Dynamics of Creation*

'Through the window watched a couple of planes leaping and looping in the blue air like dolphins. Perfect symbol for freedom.'

Arthur Koestler, writer; from his prison diary written while he was awaiting execution during the Spanish Civil War. *See* Symbols.

Radio head, China, 2006 (above)
A scene from China in 2006.

Dog splash (left)
A dog found in a splash of paint on a London wall.

Radio Times head (bottom left)
A scene from Stroud, UK, 2009.

Lipstick collar (bottom right)
A lipstick kiss on a collar inspired this witty shirt.

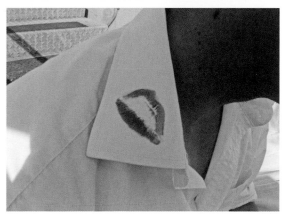

 DIY
Always carry a digital or mobile phone camera to record the visual treasures you find in the street, at work or at play. The quality of the camera is unimportant; it's what you photograph that matters: the manhole cover that looks like a football, the painted yellow lines in the road that look like a face, the serendipitous shadow in an unexpected shape. *See* Happy accidents. Use your photographs as an ideas resource. *See* Sketchbooks and scrapbooks.

 Brainjack
It can be very exciting to find an idea. Share your discoveries by communicating the thrill to others.

Flags

For thousands of years flags have been used to convey messages that indicate membership of a tribe, army, religion, city or nation. They have been a source of inspiration for many designers, photographers, film-makers and artists, including Robert Frank, Robert Mapplethorpe and the Pop artists.

F

Flags

Rooney NIKE flag (right)
Footballer Wayne Rooney creates a passionate human English flag of St George in this 2006 campaign for NIKE created by ad agency Wieden and Kennedy.

Union Jack swastika (right below)
A 2002 campaign to stamp out racism on UK University campuses created for the UK National Union of Students by ad agency Bartle Bogle Hegarty. *See* Torn Images and Tension between words and images.

Liu Yizhong, *Impressions of Britain* **(opposite)**
Plaited and parted hair create the Union Jack in this poster created for an exhibition of work by Chinese students showcasing their impressions of the UK.

JUST DO IT

RACISM TEARS BRITAIN APART.

Semaphore
The Beatles appropriated the semaphore flag-signalling system for the cover of their album *Help!*, though for some reason the letters that are spelt out are N-U-J-V.

Sending messages

Coloured flags were once used to send messages between distant ships at sea. Today, some information signalled with flags is still easily understood: a flag at half-mast indicates a recent death or a period of mourning; waving a white flag signifies surrender or a call for truce; a red flag warns of danger; and a string of small flags or bunting is a sign of celebration.

Other flags convey commonly known meanings. A skull and crossbones communicates a buccaneering spirit or piracy and is often manipulated to illustrate copyright piracy issues and articles about pirate radio, while a chequered flag is a universal symbol of motor racing. *See* Symbols.

The messages created by flags can mean different things to different audiences. For example, youthful viewers of *Easy Rider* saw the motorcycle that was decorated with the stars and stripes as symbolizing freedom, while for an older generation it signalled degeneracy. In the 1970s when Jamie Reid, Malcolm McLaren and Vivienne Westwood used the Union Jack flag in publicity and clothing for the Sex Pistols, similar tensions were created.

For young fans it signalled the dawn of a new era while it greatly offended many people who still stood to attention when the national anthem was played after cinema screenings and performances in theatres.

Flying colours

Designer Ken Garland was inspired by Japan's long, thin banners when he created the design for the flags that were used during a demonstration by the Campaign for Nuclear Disarmament (CND). He contacted every branch of CND throughout the United Kingdom: 'We bought sets of stencils about 18 inches [45 centimetres] high and told all the branches in the country that these were available and had to be used with white paint, on black cloth of a certain weight and length on a pole of a certain height and diameter. They could write whatever they liked – their name or a slogan.' When the hundreds of tall flags came collectively together the effect was amazing. Garland's idea of utilizing the power of flags created a dramatic and harmonized identity for the demonstration. *See* Garage genius.

IMPRESSIONS OF BRITAIN
PHOTOGRAPHY BY STUDENTS FROM
SUZHOU ART AND DESIGN TECHNOLOGY INSTITUTE
PRIVATE VIEW FRI 30th MAY 6pm - 9pm PUBLIC VIEW SAT 31st MAY - THURS 05th JUNE 10AM - 4PM

英国学生的中国印象
中国学生的英国印象

National flags

National flags were the world's first logos. They are globally understood and are used in the pageants and rituals of every country.

Raising the flag

Raising a flag signifies victory or ownership and is the subject of some of the world's most famous photographs, such as the one of Neil Armstrong planting the United States flag on the moon. Another is *Old Glory Goes Up on Mt. Suribachi*; Joe Rosenthal's image of United States troops claiming victory on the tiny island of Iwo Jima in February 1945 was the inspiration for the life-size Marine Corps monument in Washington and three Hollywood films. Numerous designers, cartoonists and illustrators have used the photograph, including Matt Groening for a scene in *The Simpsons* and, in London, the graffiti artist Banksy. *See* Photographs.

Russia has its own version of 'Old Glory', photographed only two months later by Yevgeny Khaldei. A Red Army sergeant raises the red flag among the statues on the roof of the Reichstag in Berlin as the city burns below. It is perhaps more powerful than Rosenthal's photograph as it symbolizes the final fall of the Nazi regime – though the message was totally muddied when, on close inspection, it was spotted that the sergeant was wearing two watches, revealing the looting that was common in war. Stalin swiftly had the photograph retouched to remove one of them.

Rallying to the flag

Flags are hugely powerful and emotive. After the attack on the Twin Towers in 2001 the entire population of the United States seemed to turn to their flag for comfort and reassurance.

The American flag is a brilliant design, both representational and symbolic. The white stars on a blue background record the number of states and also suggest the heavens; the stripes and the lack of a centre indicate harmony and democracy. In 1958 when the United States embraced two additional states there was a nationwide competition to redesign the flag. A high school student, Robert G. Heft, simply redrew the flag with 50 stars instead of the former 48, and received a B+ from his teacher as his design 'lacked originality'. Despite this knock-back the design won the competition and Heft went on to become a successful politician.

The depth of emotion that is invested in flags can be seen in the fact that setting fire to a nation's flag is seen as the highest insult.

Flag waving

Flags are widely used in propaganda at times of war and revolution. They featured prominently in the art, design, films and songs of all sides in the First and Second World Wars, and in the Russian and Chinese revolutions.

Propaganda images are an amazing source of inspiration, often featuring huge rescaling of faces and objects. *See* Rescaling.

Chinese flag
Photographer Pete Bedwell recreated the Chinese flag using people for the stars in this image used for posters and fliers promoting a series of exhibitions staged in China by UK students.

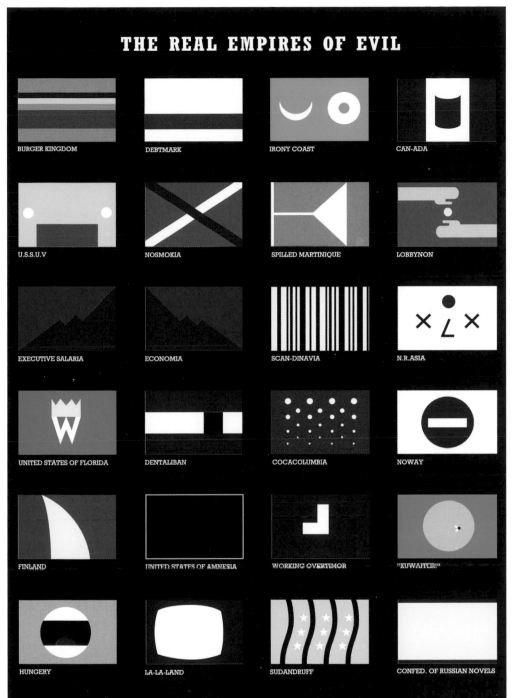

THE REAL EMPIRES OF EVIL

BURGER KINGDOM

DEBTMARK

IRONY COAST

CAN-ADA

U.S.S.U.V

NOSMOKIA

SPILLED MARTINIQUE

LOBBYNON

EXECUTIVE SALARIA

ECONOMIA

SCAN-DINAVIA

N.R.ASIA

UNITED STATES OF FLORIDA

DENTALIBAN

COCACOLUMBIA

NOWAY

FINLAND

UNITED STATES OF AMNESIA

WORKING OVERTIMOR

"KUWAITER!"

HUNGERY

LA-LA-LAND

SUDANDRUFF

CONFED. OF RUSSIAN NOVELS

Christoph Niemann, *The Real Empires of Evil* (above)
Christoph Niemann is immensely playful with the simple graphic language of flags in these witty illustrations.
See www.christophniemann.com

FRENCH MARKET

Market stalls and street entertainment from France

Thursday 12 & Friday 13 October
Wembley Town Centre
High Road Wembley by Argos

Saturday 14 & Sunday 15 October
Willesden Town Centre
Outside Willesden Green Library Centre

9am – 6pm

020 8937 5323
www.wembleytown.com
www.willesdentown.com

SUPPORTED BY
LONDON
DEVELOPMENT
AGENCY
WORKING FOR THE MAYOR OF LONDON

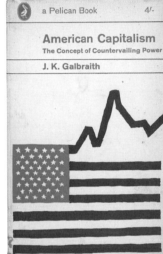

a Pelican Book 4/-

American Capitalism
The Concept of Countervailing Power

J. K. Galbraith

French Garlic (top)
Poster for a French market opening in London fusing two symbols of France – the Tricolor flag and a clove of garlic. Design by Alistair Hall at design group We Made This.
See Symbols and www.wemadethis.co.uk

Pelican book (above)
A wavering stripe from the American flag reflects the ups and downs of US prosperity in this book cover. The two words of the title are represented by a single simple image.

DIY
The simple graphic quality and use of bold colour in the design of flags means they are instantly recognizable, no matter how severely they have been cropped, distorted or manipulated. They can be used to express powerful messages, both positive and negative.

Brainjack
The bold design and colour intrinsic to flags together with the powerful emotions woven into many can make them magnetic both to the eye and to the heart.

Fusion

Fusion is the creative merging, blending or combination of two or more unexpected and previously unrelated elements. Fashion designers, in particular, love fusion. Jean Paul Gaultier's 2010 collection was described as Aztecs meets Avatar, while Givenchy's collection was Emmanuelle meets Bowie. *Film directors pitch their ideas as fusions. For example, the British animator Nick Park described his idea for* Chicken Run *as 'The Great Escape – with chickens'.*

'Actually, Michelangelo and Muybridge are mixed up in my mind together.'

Francis Bacon, artist

Jonathan Barnbrook, *Rosama McLaden*, 2003 (above)
Designer Barnbrook's Bin-Mac combo. *See* www.barnbrook.net

Brilliant chairs (right)
Italian artist and designer Martino Gamper fused antique and modern chairs, mixing inexpensive and vastly expensive elements to produce these witty hybrids. *See* www.gampermartino.com

'Teenage Psycho Meets Bloody Mary'

Title of 1950s trash movie.
See **So bad it's good.**

 DIY
Fuse, blend and cross-pollinate your sources of inspiration. Find startling new combinations.

 Brainjack
New cross-pollinations can create unexpected hybrids that bloom in the mind of the viewer.

F

Fusion

G

Garage genius

Having no money, no budget or no computer is no barrier to communication. When German-born artist Kurt Schwitters was imprisoned in Douglas Camp on the Isle of Man during the Second World War he turned his room into a studio. Here – to the amazement of his guards – he created sculptures from porridge and made prints using stolen pieces of lino tile. Ideas created with even very little money can be hugely impactful.

Hornsey 1968, (above)
A linocut poster from the famous 1968 sit-in at Hornsey College of Art in London designed by Martin Walker – its hard, carved crudity makes it compelling.

Sniffin' Glue (right)
Cover of *Sniffin' Glue*, Britain's first punk rock fanzine, created by Mark Perry in 1976. Its bold, felt-penned lettering and punchy black and white photocopied production communicate the excitement of the punk scene it heralded.

Samizdat: clandestine communication
Samizdat comes from the Russian for self-publishing, and describes work produced and disseminated by an underground press. In Soviet countries in the 1950s to 1980s many books were banned by the state and the work of creative writers, including novelists and poets, was suppressed. Freethinkers published books secretly and reproduced outlawed writing on any printing press they could get hold of, or by typing them out using carbon paper to make extra copies. Some works were written out by hand. Copies were passed from hand to hand in great secrecy as discovery meant instant arrest and imprisonment. This highly potent clandestine communication helped to undermine the Soviet Union's oppressive regime.

Photographers Pierre et Gilles were inspired by seeing, in India, what they called 'the thing of making the marvellous with nothing, with planks of wood and papier-mâché'. Imagination and making the most of what is to hand can help the most ambitious of ideas to come to fruition. As a young photographer Cecil Beaton made fantastic studio sets for his portraits out of practically nothing. He created swirling sets from torn paper and cheap fabrics, seascapes from old tarpaulins and improvised a striking, patterned backdrop from an upturned old bedstead he found on the street. Beaton used his photographic skills to distil magical images from these basic materials.

Film director Garth Jennings created a wonderful, silent chase movie in a blacked-out room with hand-held torches to illuminate the characters – the drama was created solely through the framing and acting, and the movement of the camera.

Crayon power

The simple pencil or wax crayon can be an extraordinarily powerful communication tool, as seen in James Victore's hand-drawn images which roar angrily at viewers to take notice. Abram Games drew all his posters, including the lettering, by hand. He never resorted to using photography or typesetting. He summarized his approach as 'minimum means, maximum impact'.

Raw communication

The stark, inky black-and-white posters, silk-screened by hand, used in the Paris student riots of 1968, and the duplicated and linocut posters of the London art school protests of the same year possess a potent, raw quality because of the swiftness and cheapness of their production. The London protests were nicknamed the 'Gestetner revolution' after the stencil duplicating machine used to create pamphlets and posters for demonstrations and meetings.

The badly photocopied punk artwork and fanzines of 1976/77 have the same kind of visual vigour. They look like vital messages from the front line, urgently appealing to viewers to storm the barricades.

Images created with hand-cut stencils and spray paint can have a similar character.

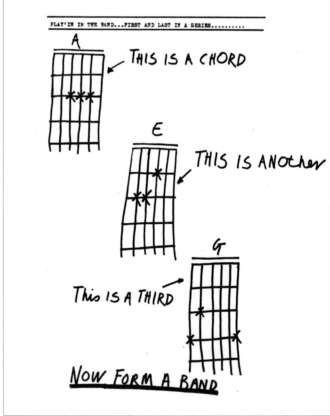

'Gentlemen, we don't have any money so we're going to have to think.'

Ernest Rutherford, 'the father of modern physics'

'Imagination costs nothing.'

Jonathan Meades, writer

'Ideas created with low budgets seem far more pure.'

Bohnchang Koo, artist

'There's no passion in pixels. Say goodbye to the sterility of the computer; the tools of really powerful communication are the scalpel, the stencil and the spray can.'

Schway Whar, designer

'Designing without a computer really forces you to focus on the job in hand.'

Arnaud Marquoin-Seignolles, designer and teacher

'A project made with love rather than money is wonderful.'

Julian Temple, film-maker

'Korean art and design features the skills of the hand. There is something courageous and compelling about seeing a mark that has been made only once – digital work never has this potency.'

Bohnchang Koo, artist

DIY
Let your imagination overcome budgetary constraints. Use the tools you have at hand rather than those you ideally wish to have.

Embrace the handcrafted. Get your hands dirty. Try crayon, pencil and stencil power. Discover or rediscover the pleasure of making, drawing, folding, tearing and cutting. Draw in other ways – with a sewing machine, for example, or with light in long-exposure photographs. *See* Photography.

Collect and study folk design, like sports fans' banners and the home-made ones that welcome loved ones at airports, and hand-drawn and hand-painted signs and announcements.

Experiment with easily accessible and inexpensive ways to create and reproduce images, such as by using the scanner, photocopier or camera phone.

Try spreading hand-made messages from hand to hand like *samizdat* (see page 69) This means of dissemination is personal, and because it can feel both illicit and exciting it makes communication memorable.

Paris SS (opposite left)
An incredibly provocative and impactful anti-police poster produced to be fly-posted and carried in demonstrations during the 1968 anti-government protests in Paris. It was designed and screen-printed by the creative workshop known as Atelier Populaire.

Tony Moon, ...*Now Form a Band*, *Sideburns* fanzine,1977 (opposite right)
A hastily scribbled page from another 1970s fanzine that perfectly encapsulates the early spirit of punk. The message is simple, empowering and urgent – join in now, it's really easy, just do it yourself.

johnson banks, Recycled xmas cards (above and right)
A studio Christmas card from the London-based design group johnson banks, hand punched from magazines and brochures found around the office. Cost – zilch, idea – fantastic. Their message to their clients – Happy Christmas + we're smart and we recycle. Designers Michael Johnson, Pali Palavathanan and Miho Aishima.
See www.johnsonbanks.co.uk

Brainjack
Something that is hand-made, hand-drawn, home-made, cheaply produced and hand distributed can communicate on a powerfully intimate and personal level. In our screen-saturated world hand-made things can convey messages at a highly visceral level.

Further viewing
The brilliant Oscar-winning film-maker Nick Park is a master of handcrafting and making the most with the least. All the characters in his brilliant Wallace and Gromit animated films are created by hand in plasticine – it is wonderful that, now and again, a thumb print can be spotted.

H

Hands

You can solve any brief with an image of hands. Handprints were the first marks early humans left on the walls of caves. Way before we had learnt to make drawings with tools we could make patterns with our muddy hands.

Everyone has individual hand- and fingerprints. They are a record of our uniqueness, used both by police to identify criminals and to celebrate achievement and fame when celebrities press their hands into wet cement in public ceremonies in Hollywood.

F. H. K. Henrion, Poster for the United States Office of War Information, 1944
Four hands representing the nations of Russia, US, France and Britain smash fascism. Henrion was born in Germany, trained in Paris and emigrated to England in the 1930s, adopting British nationality. He was a hugely influential designer in the 1940s and 50s.

U.S.P.F.11.

Gestures: visual shorthand

Hand gestures are an ancient means of human communication used in every culture. There are local differences in what they mean and a gesture in one country can have an opposite meaning in another one – something that has been used in advertising campaigns and posters, and has caused great problems for hitch-hikers.

The victory V-sign has been used by prime ministers, presidents, soldiers and sportsmen, and is universal. It is common in snapshots of young people, particularly in Japan. It became the signature gesture of both Nixon and Churchill. Nixon preferred a version with both hands upwardly outstretched while Churchill gave the V-sign with his fingers facing either front or back – though the usual interpretation of the forward-facing V is that it is abusive.

When sportsman Harvey Smith gave the forward V-sign gesture to judges after winning a showjumping competition they refused to give him the prize money. He took them to court and smartly won the cash after showing Churchill using both variations of the sign to indicate victory. 'Doing a Harvey Smith' became a popular term and has entered the dictionary to describe the gesture.

The 'bunny ears' version of the sign, where the fingers are held behind an unsuspecting person's head, is commonplace in photographs.

Gang signs

Racetrack bookmakers and city traders have evolved a series of hand signals to communicate the changing prices offered by rivals. The racing gestures, known as tic-tac, clearly communicate complex messages across long distances in the chaotic atmosphere of a racecourse, though they are dying out as a means of communication, replaced by mobile phones.

The military, street gangs and secret societies such as the Mafia and the Freemasons also have hand-signal languages to communicate greetings and warnings, while officials in many team sports convey decisions to both players and spectators through hand gestures.

Peter Kennard, *Crushed Missile*, 1980 (above)
Artist Kennard created this image for the UK Campaign for Nuclear Disarmament using a powerful man's hand to symbolize 'the people', who if unified, could rid the country of nuclear weapons. In crushing the missile the hand makes the clenched fist gesture – used to express defiance, solidarity and strength. *See* Symbols, www.peterkennard.com.

Nelson Mandela, *Hand of Africa*, charity artwork, 2003 (right)
This handprint with a map of Africa within the palm of the former South African president made front-page news around the world. Reputedly created unconsciously while Mandela made paintings for an auction aimed at raising awareness and money for his charity helping HIV sufferers, this handy accident achieved both.

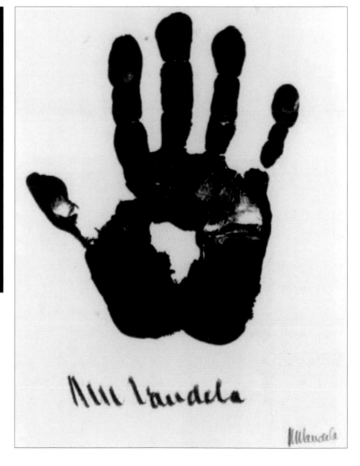

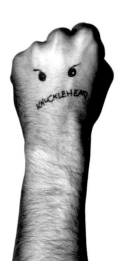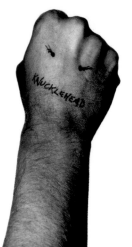

Knucklehead identity (top)
An identity for London-based ad, film, promo and viral production company Knucklehead featuring the hands of each director. Designed by Michael Johnson and Kath Tudball from Design group johnson banks. *See* www.johnsonbanks.co.uk.

Hand chair (above)
A chair inspired by a gloved hand, seen in a fast food restaurant in Beijing, China. It is inspired by an earlier sofa known as the 'Joe' sofa – created to look like a massive baseball glove and named after baseball legend Joe DiMaggio. The sofa was designed in 1970 by Italians Jonathan De Pas, Donato D'Urbino and Paulo Lomazzi who in turn were inspired by Claes Oldenburg's massively rescaled objects. *See* Rescaling.

Hand carved (right)
Handprints found on walls in Malta.

DIY

Use the expressive quality of hands to communicate your ideas. They can convey complex ideas in a way that viewers can easily understand. Aggression and strength, friendship and community, despair, pain and pleasure can be shown simply with images featuring hands.

Examine hand signals that are related to the message you wish to communicate.

Brainjack

The power of engagement of certain gestures is deeply imprinted in everyone. Some, such as the outstretched finger pointed at the viewer, are so commanding they draw us to an image with irresistible force. This use of the hand was seen in the famous British recruiting poster for World War I, designed by Alfred Leete. Its success inspired numerous other warring nations to produce posters demanding that men join their armies. *See* Torn images.

Superdry counting to ten

Photographer Leanne Newcombe uses the Chinese hand gestures from ten down to one in a poster promoting the countdown to the launch of Superdry clothing in China.

Happy accidents

In the commercial production of china and pottery, plates stacked in kilns for firing occasionally collapse, distort and fuse together. They are nicknamed wasters and can be strikingly beautiful – an example is displayed in the Victoria & Albert Museum in London. Appreciate these happy accidents – don't let the wasters go to waste. See Museums.

An unwasted waster (right)
This amazing waster was created in a happy accident around 350 years ago.

Ron Arad, Babyboop vase, 2002 (opposite)
Arad accidentally discovered the process used to make these beautiful vases by inflating sheets of metal while on a factory visit. *See* www.ronarad.co.uk

Travelling to new worlds
Happy accidents can lead creative people in previously unthought-of directions. While artist and photographer Man Ray was working in his darkroom the door was accidentally opened, allowing daylight to spill on to the prints in the developing tray. He thought his pictures were ruined, but found that they were magically transformed to part-positive, part-negative images as a result of being exposed to light during processing. Ray embraced his new-found technique and revelled in its unpredictability.

Divine accidents
Artist Andy Warhol called examples of chance creativity 'divine accidents'. He exhibited all the 'mistakes' that were accidentally created when the silk screens used to produce his work became clogged with ink, as he felt they added to the quality of the images.

Go to the factory
Always visit the factory, manufacturer or printer involved in your project. On the surface these visits may seem boring, but once you get there you will often find great inspiration; something quite wonderful may be in a skip or bin, or leaning against the wall. It could be a misprint, an overprint, a reject, a test, miscutting, a bit cut off in finishing or an accident. When you ask what it is, you'll be told: 'You can't be interested in that. We're going to throw it away – it was a mistake.' But to you it will be inspirational treasure, a happy accident that inspires new thinking and ideas.

DIY
Appreciate serendipitous mistakes; they can have a unique quality that is beyond the norm.

Brainjack
A mistake can seem special, in the way misprinted stamps and mispressed coins are highly prized. A mistake defies the norm. It can jar and be memorable – it is unusual and unexpected in that it has escaped quality control.

Hidden messages

Messages can be deliberately concealed, hidden in different ways. They can be designed to be discovered by accident or uncovered only by a viewer who is actively searching for them. Or they may be readable only if imagery or a code known by a select audience is used. Uncovering a hidden message creates a sensation of revelation.

Margaux Luzuriaga, *wallpaper*, 2005
At first sight, this wallpaper, created by Margaux Luzuriaga appears tastefully patterned and ideal for any suburban front room. On closer inspection, it is something else entirely.

Targeting an audience of one
When designer Paul Rand was pitching for work from the music giant RCA he knew that communicating to the very top boss of the company was the key. Realizing that his target had once been a wireless operator, Rand took a full-page advertisement in *The New York Times* and used hugely enlarged Morse code symbols for the letters R, C and A for the decorative elements. He said: 'I knew that a million eyes might see the copy of *The Times*; the only eyes that mattered were his.' He got the job.

Hidden messages on television

When *Melrose Place* was launched as a spin-off from the appalling high school drama *Beverly Hills 90210* it looked like any other trashy Hollywood soap opera featuring a cast of bland wooden actors with fake tans. It struggled to find an audience and was soon cancelled because of poor ratings.

The show is brilliant. Unnoticed, under the surface there are numerous provocative hidden messages that deal with issues banned from the airwaves by television legislation. Interiors, props and clothing feature images and slogans that add an entirely new layer to the drama by offering a parallel, hidden commentary on the soap opera's plot. For example, although the teenage bed-hopping characters never ever discuss safe sex their duvets and pillows are printed with hundreds of condoms.

Other issues highlighted by hidden messages include police brutality, the omnipresence of guns, abortion and racism. Comments on the anaesthetizing effect of television, and even a T-shirt stating 'Censorship is un-American' sneaked past the television censors.

This extraordinary project was created by the artist Mel Chin, with students at the University of Georgia and the University of California, Santa Barbara, in a secret collaboration with Deborah Siegel, the show's set designer.

Cult messages

In the 1970s the punk band the Sex Pistols advertised their early concerts with a series of black-and-white photocopied A4 collages. Inspired by the Dada movement, they used crude typography made from random letters cut from daily newspapers. This gave the fliers – then known as handbills – the feel of ransom notes from criminals or freedom fighters. They were radically different from all other contemporary messages, and drew blank stares from everyone except those in the know about this then tiny musical cult. Writer Jon Savage wrote that, 'like communiqués, the Sex Pistols' handbills spoke in codes to the initiated only'.

In the 1980s designer Peter Saville aimed to create what he called a 'mass-produced secret' in his design of the packaging for the bands he worked with in Manchester. He bucked the norm by not showing photographs of the groups, the album title or even a list the songs. For one album he used a colour-based code to hide all the information about the band on the front, with a decoding key on the back. He reused the code on later records so that only fans who were in the know about it could understand the messages hidden in the colours.

Sparkling messages

While sporting an engagement or wedding ring is a commonly understood public statement of commitment and unavailability, historically other messages that can be decoded only by wearers or recipients who know the meanings allotted to different gems and designs have been concealed within jewellery. Rubies represent passion, emeralds hope, sapphires repentance or loyalty, and amethysts devotion. The initial letters of the gemstones are sometimes used in a design spell out messages. For example, a brooch featuring diamonds, emeralds, amethysts and rubies spells out D-E-A-R. Different shapes have different meanings: a snake symbolizes eternity and an anchor hope and steadfastness, while clasped hands mean friendship.

Hiding from the police

When Andy Warhol was inspired to create some pornographic paintings he was fearful that any exhibition of the pictures would be raided by the police and he would be thrown in jail. He had the brilliant idea of using ultraviolet inks to silk-screen the images on to white canvases so that they were visible only when illuminated with ultraviolet bulbs. If the police arrived the paintings could be hidden by turning off the bulbs that made them visible. The normal lights simply showed gallery-goers gathered around a series of blank canvases. Once the police had gone Warhol would be able to reveal the paintings again to the delight of his friends.

Hidden linings

The clothes we wear convey messages about our occupation, status, wealth and aspirations. They identify the tribe we belong to and there are strict conventions in the dress of every social group from Goths to city workers. We make instant judgements based on clothing when we encounter a new person, a fact exploited by Paul Smith when he designed hidden messages within his clothes. Conventionally cut, sober suits and ties hide vividly coloured and patterned linings – a glimpse of which contradicts the first impression that wearers of the suits are conservative and dull.

Clandestine mass communication

In the 1960s many music fans believed secret messages were contained within albums, either concealed in the images on the sleeves or accessible only by playing the records backwards or at different speeds. Some messages were smuggled on to records, inscribed on the vinyl at the end of the grooves on one side.

The Freemasons – who greet each other with secret handshakes – created what are perhaps the world's biggest hidden messages within the city of Bath in the west of England. Giant symbols, only visible from the air, are built into its streets and parks, their meanings known only to Freemasons.

Hair dryer/light activated (above)
Heat and UV light reveal imagery hidden within these designs.

'We were asked to design a sleeve for a recording made at a secret gig. The design came totally out of this idea of secrecy. We created a sleeve featuring a "wordsearch" in which all the information is hidden. You can find out where the gig was, who plays what instrument, the week, the month, the year, even the weather at the time.'

Rebecca and Mike, multidisciplinary designers

DIY
Secrete messages in your work.

 Brainjack
The accidental discovery of a hidden form of communication can bring a jolt of revelation to the viewer, while interacting with a message to uncover information through a search can be highly rewarding.

Hidden and coded messages create an exciting collusion between the creator and those who are in the know as to how they can be deciphered. The viewer who receives and understands them is thrilled and excited to be included in an elite group. It is like being in an exclusive club whose members communicate only on a certain wavelength; they alone can understand what is being said because they are able to think at that frequency.

Humour

Humorous messages amuse viewers, provoking inner smiles and lifting the spirits. Humour creates a bond between the creator and recipient at the instant when the viewer gets the joke – there is appreciation for the cleverness of the message and satisfaction that this has been spotted. It is an intimate form of communication; comedian Victor Borge commented: 'Humour is the shortest distance between two people.'

In his foreword to A Smile in the Mind Edward de Bono commented that, 'humour is the exact model of creativity. In both we access from the far end of the pattern that which cannot be accessed from the near end.' This is demonstrated in the old joke: 'Getting off the underground train I saw a sign saying "Dogs must be carried on the escalator" – it took me an hour to find one.'

Pouring water joke sequence (right)
Art students Laura Moody and Zoe Shannon created this sequence in response to the project 'Tell a joke in six images'.

'Humour is a means of establishing good will, good fellowship, confidence and the right frame of mind towards an idea or product.'

Paul Rand, designer

'People like fun. If you're trying to get people to try new things, they're far more likely to try it if it's fun.'

Espen Sivertsen, social innovation teacher

DIY
Humour me! Generate ideas that communicate through fun.

Brainjack
Humour engages by entertaining and causing amusement, which creates a feeling of warmth in the viewer's mind. The reward for the creator is that in exchange for being entertained audiences pay attention to the message.

Icons

The word icon was first used to describe a holy picture worshipped by believers. It has now come to mean someone or something that is universally and uncritically admired with an equivalent level of adoration.

FIRST SHOWING OF A NEW POLAROID LAND FILM. This is an enlargement of an actual 60-second picture of Louis Armstrong. It was taken with a new film, just introduced, which is twice as sharp as the previous film.

With this latest development, the Polaroid Land Camera not only gives you pictures in 60 seconds, but pictures of exceptional clarity and brilliance. Polaroid Land Cameras start at $72.75. The new film can be identified by a star on the box.

Human icons

Iconic status has been achieved only by an exclusive few individuals. While the fame of the vast majority of those known as celebrities wilts swiftly, that of true icons continues to grow even long after they have died. Icons are immortal and, no matter how much we are told about their imperfections, their status is unchanged in our minds. Icons are more than national treasures; they are world treasures.

The power of their status can been seen in the fact that, like deities, many icons are known throughout the world by a single name: Einstein, Marilyn, Ali, Pelé, Elvis, Gandhi, Che and Picasso. They have been described as the saints of our secular age and Marilyn is even known a 'goddess'.

Instant icons

The best-known photographs of icons are simple, pared-down images, often in black and white. Examples are Che wearing a beret with a revolutionary star, Einstein poking his tongue out and Audrey Hepburn in close-up holding a long cigarette holder. This visual language inspired the poster for the film *Trainspotting*, where instantly iconic images of its young stars were created in a series of animated black-and-white photographs of the characters 'cut out' on white backgrounds. The images were described by the film's director as imbuing the actors with a 'defiant swagger'. The *Trainspotting* poster is now Blu-Tacked to the bedroom walls of many teenagers alongside photographs of the icons than inspired it.

French photographers Pierre et Gilles are inspired by religious icons. They use the way they are composed, and their poses and bright gaudy colours, for portraits of pop and film stars. *See* Places of worship.

Design icons

Certain designs such as the London Underground map and the 'I ❤ New York' logo have been promoted to iconic status. Like human icons, these have gained a special place in the public's heart.

The icon business

The powerful effect that recognizing the few people deemed truly iconic has on the public has led to their images being highly valuable in advertising. To prevent a free-for-all, international laws have been introduced that prohibit commercial use of an icon's photograph without permission. These laws have granted what are called image rights to icons – meaning they have been given the right to commercially market and sell their image as only they think fit.

Icons are now fiercely protected. This is the responsibility of their management when they are alive and of their descendants when they die. Any potential use of an image in advertising is carefully vetted to ensure the icon's status is not diluted and devalued by association with an inferior product or service. Ownership of an icon's image rights can now be bought and sold like any other commodity. Muhammad Ali's were recently auctioned for millions of dollars.

Iconic ads (opposite)
In the 1999 ads (opposite far left) Apple computers use the iconic status of Picasso and the Dalai Lama to send the message that they too are visionary thinkers. Louis Armstrong, the personification of creative joy, features in the 1958 ad for Polaroid cameras (opposite right).

Lorenzo Agius, *Trainspotting*, movie poster, 1996 (right)
Photographer Lorenzo Agius shot the young, unknown *Trainspotting* actors in the dynamic, high-impact, black and white visual style seen in many famous images of icons.

Iconic vs celebrity endorsement

Celebrities can be mistaken for icons, but no matter how carefully they nurture their public persona to create a good image they lack the latter's invulnerability. Icons are totally trusted while celebrities can prove untrustworthy. This was seen in the midst of a campaign created for the razor company Gillette in which golfer Tiger Woods and footballer Thierry Henry endorsed its products in advertisements. Both had been chosen for their clean-cut wholesomeness but Woods was a serial wife-cheater and Henry was accused of handling the ball. Their reputations are forever damaged.

Simon Patterson, *The Great Bear*, 1992 (below)
Harry Beck's London Underground map has become a much-loved design icon and symbol of London since its creation in the 1930s – *see* Science, Symbols. Like the 'I ❤ New York' rebus it is printed on T-shirts, posters, mugs, mouse mats and numerous other types of merchandise and has inspired the design of maps for transport systems throughout the world. Its coloured arteries, sequences of stations and intersections are deeply imprinted in the minds of millions of users. Artist Patterson's redesign replaces the station names with those of comedians, footballers, actors, scientists, saints, philosophers, politicians, explorers and planets arranged along each different track, stations wittily fit or jar with the names with which they have been replaced. Patterson's use of the iconic map allows viewers to take wonderful new journeys in their imaginations travelling back and forth through history, culture and space.

FREE EVERY WEEK! New bumper sport section inside

ShortList

WWW.SHORTLIST.COM   EVERY THURSDAY

Enter the
O₂ X Awards.
Win £5,000!

TEVEZ LEADS THE REVOLUTION

An exclusive interview with
the man spearheading Manchester
City's Premier League assault

ISSUE 91 / 30 JULY 2009

Tevez as Che, magazine cover (left)
Che symbolizes youthful rebellion, a dream of progress and revolution, in this award-winning magazine cover Argentinian footballer Carlos Tevez becomes the icon – communicating that the maverick striker has been signed in the hope of bringing glory to a football club stuck in the doldrums.

Audrey Hepburn, LG phones ad (bottom left)
Audrey Hepburn's image as Holly Golightly confers style on a brand of mobile phones in this ad seen in the Chinese metro.

James Dean Converse ad (bottom right)
Iconic film star James Dean – the embodiment of youthful rebellion – perfectly fills the shoes of someone needed to advertise iconic Converse footwear.

DIY
Find a connection between your project or brief and an icon, then develop and maximize the interrelationship.
See Music, Movies.

Brainjack
Icons are mesmerizing. They never date. Pictures of icons are speedily 'read' by viewers as fame and renown are compellingly compressed in their images. Icons are highly effective in communication to mass audiences as they instantly symbolize values that are profoundly understood by every viewer. For example, Audrey Hepburn = stylish beauty, Che and James Dean = youthful rebellion, Picasso = visionary artistic genius and Marilyn = glamour. *See* Symbols.

Icons are not totally untouchable. The portrayal of an icon or iconic image in an unexpected manner is striking. It provokes a powerful response as an image with a precious status that has been tampered with.

Illusion

An illusion is something that deceives the eye and thereby tricks the mind. Illusions turn twist, spin and throb in the mind of the viewer.

It is said that the greatest thing a designer can do is 'buy' the time of the consumer. As illusions make viewers double-take, perhaps they dwell on them for double the time that would be given to a conventional image – in which case illusions are twice as potent as other means of communicating.

Illusions are compelling; they exploit the space between the eye and the brain. The brain tries to insist that the visual clues it has been given must be believed, and for the viewer this creates the exciting experience of feeling they can't believe their eyes – which they normally trust entirely.

Double Take
A visual surprise awaits when this page is turned upside down. This two-faced character was drawn by an Italian artist called Giuseppe around three hundred years ago as a 'memento mori' – a reminder to viewers that we are all mortal.

'When you see something that is literally amazing, you can't believe your eyes, it's magical. That work inspires me.'
Ross Cooper,
multidisciplinary designer

Bridget Riley, *Blaze 4*, 1963 (above)
British artist Bridget Riley's 1963 painting
Blaze 4 creates optical sensations so intense
that it can be disorientating to view.

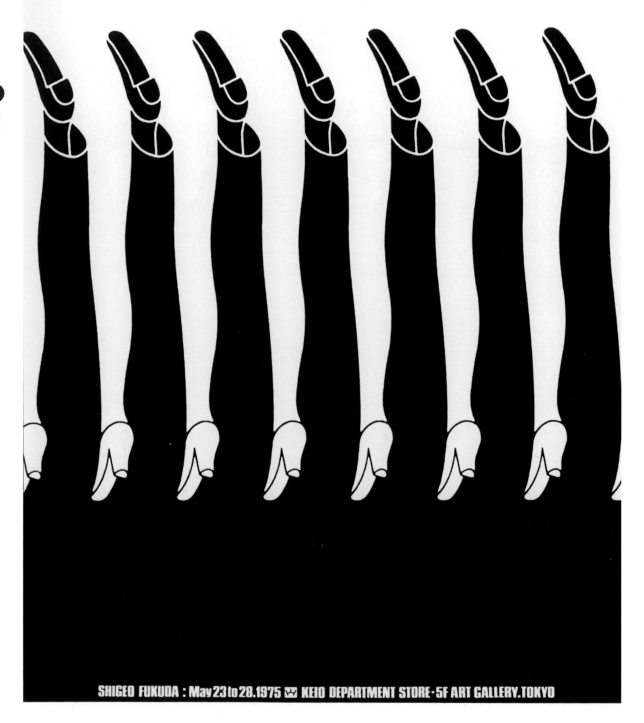

SHIGEO FUKUDA : May 23 to 28.1975 [logo] KEIO DEPARTMENT STORE·5F ART GALLERY.TOKYO

Shigeo Fukuda, *Legs Dancing* (opposite)
Japanese artist, designer and master visual illusionist Shigeo Fukuda created this poster in which men and women's legs dance together in the mind. *See* Shadows.

Calum Colvin, *Natural Magick* (right)
Scottish artist Calum Colvin's masterful images combine construction, painting and photography. He paints onto the surfaces of carefully assembled groups of objects to create the illusion of a two-dimensional drawing only visible at a single viewpoint – from which he then photographs. The pictures appear simultaneously both flat and three-dimensional.
See www.calumcolvin.com

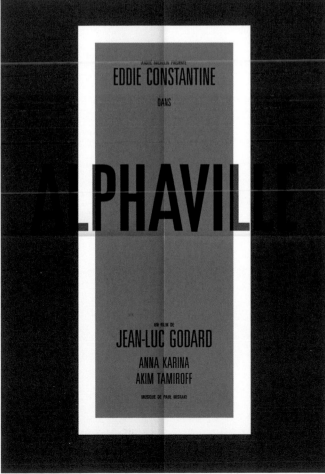

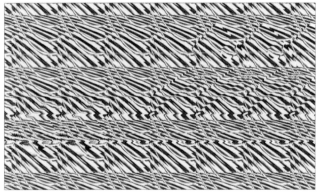

LOOK CLOSELY FOR THE KEY TO THE RIGHT MORTGAGE

Magic Eye Key ad (above)
Ad for Lloyds bank created in 1995 at the height of the craze for these 'magic eye' pictures. To view the illusion you have to stare at the image and try to look 'past' its surface.

***Alphaville* poster (left)**
David Pearson created this contemporary poster for the 1965 French movie *Alphaville*. The design gives the illusion that the poster has been carefully folded and treasured.
See www.davidpearsondesign.com

 DIY
Be inspired by illusions. Seek ones that can deliver your message and bewitch your viewer.

 Brainjack
Creating illusions offers magic for viewers' eyes and stimulus for their minds. They can be entranced by a visual hypnotism.

Irony

An ironic use of images and words conveys a meaning that is the opposite to what is actually stated. One thing is said but the opposite is implied. To launch a new season's collection the Italian fashion company Diesel created a memorably ironic campaign: How To Do Fashion Photography. Instead of sending out the usual brochure showing beautiful models wearing outfits in beautiful locations they produced what at first glance looked like a manual showing how to take hip fashion photographs. In fact the opposite is the case.

Face value (below)

When a group of London art students wanted to attract key people from the creative industries to their graduation exhibition they came up with the slogan Same Shit Different Year. At face value the message is 'You've seen all this stuff before so you needn't bother to turn up'. The underlying message is that the show will be fresh and different. The sheer bravado and audacity of this ironic invitation demands the viewer's attendance.

How to be ironic (opposite and bottom)

Using the layout, copywriting style and typography of 'how to' manuals the creators of the Diesel brochure offered step-by-step diagrams and top tips on creating fashion photographs. The photography, poses, styling, props – and tips – are appalling. With deadpan seriousness no cliché is missed, from recommending the flagrant use of wind and smoke machines to smearing Vaseline on the camera lens to create extra-moody pictures. The first impression is that the message being communicated to a young and fashionable audience couldn't be more wrong – but this is turned on its head with the realization that the dreadful delivery is deliberate. The effect is laugh-out-loud funny. The ironic, tongue-in-cheek delivery communicates that Diesel is smart, witty and knowing. *See* So bad it's good.

DIY
Create work in which surface meaning and what lies beneath are very different.

Brainjack
'Irony purports to take seriously what it does not.'
Arthur Koestler, writer

Irony turns a message on its head by reversing its appearance. The acrobatics of this flip take place in the viewer's head. This performance in the mind can be highly entertaining.

same shit different year

Warming Up – The Stretchy Part

Before starting a photo session, it's essential to get your models in the right mood. Most are pretty stiff, but I've got some special techniques that are guaranteed to loosen them up.

a) A few simple warm-up exercises

This is actually a form of mental relaxation. Play unusual music and lead the group with a soft friendly voice.

CLOSE YOUR EYES, TAKE A DEEP BREATH AND PRETEND THAT YOU'RE GOING TO DIG INTO AN ENORMOUS APPLE PIE.

CHEW THE AIR AS YOU SLOWLY MOVE YOUR HEAD IN CIRCLES.

ON HER: JACKET 1595-BUNDLE-846 / TEE 1795-HOGEN-LIA / PANTS 1997-CHUDAN-5KT. ON HIM: TEE ZEWIA-919 / SHIRT SOM-PAC / JEANS 1196ADF-860.

WHEN TWO MODELS HAVE TO WARM UP TOGETHER, YOU'LL HAVE TO USE A COMPLETELY DIFFERENT APPROACH.

b) The mirror method

If the model is shy, get him or her to start relaxing by using the mirror method. Using this technique, the model makes sporadic movements as he or she tries to move quicker than the image in the mirror.

TOP MPL-CANASTILLA-ORF / SKIRT 132-SAMAI-INO

FOR THE MORE AMBITIOUS TYPE: THE KING FRANK TWO-MINUTES-A-DAY METHOD WILL SOON BE AVAILABLE ON VIDEO. YOU CAN ALSO DOWN-LOAD IT FROM MY WEB SITE. SURF TO WWW.KINGFRANK.COM.

c) Don't forget to relax their faces

STEP 1   STEP 2   STEP 3

SWEAT 1661-LIKANTROPO-BOT.   TOP 1888-LIWIN-SWT.   TOP 1TSU HAMIKURAI FEL.

THIS IS ONE OF MY SPECIAL FACE RELAXATION EXERCISES, IN THREE EASY STEPS.

J

Juxtaposition

To juxtapose means to put side by side. When two objects are placed together they are automatically compared. 'Before and after' images work in this way; they imply that if the viewer uses a certain product they will become thinner, less balding or have clearer skin.

johnson banks, *Britain,* **1998 (above)**
Design group johnson banks perfectly select old and new images in these posters created for the British Council. They juxtapose an evocative nostalgic black and white playground picture with an image of today's multi-racial schools and a glowing old master painting with one of Damien Hirst's dead sheep in a glass tank of formaldehyde – Hirst was at that time the *enfant terrible* of the Art World. The juxtapositions deliver a message that Britain is a place where history, tradition and vibrant modernity meet.
See www.johnsonbanks.co.uk

Nicolai Howalt, *Battered Boxer,*
2000–03 (opposite)
Danish photographer Nicolai Howalt took shots of young boxers staring straight at his camera just moments before and after fighting. The two images were displayed side by side and captioned with the result – won or lost. The juxtaposition of the fresh faces before the bout with the battered, bloodied and bruised after it, together with the knowledge of success or failure conveys to the minds of viewers the brutality of each contest. The boxer at the top won; the one below lost. Now imagine how.
See www.nicolaihowalt.com

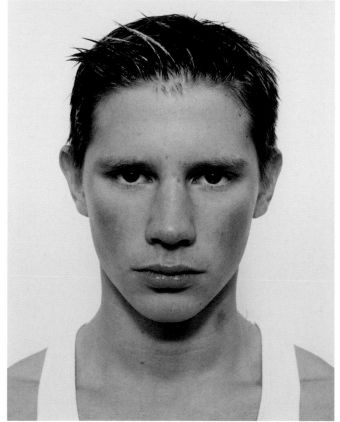
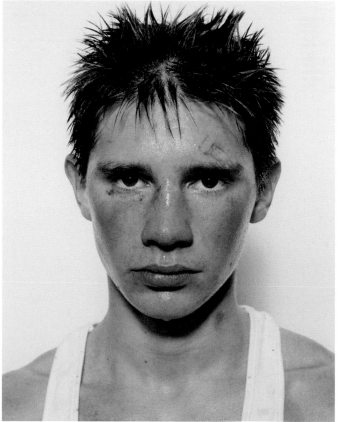

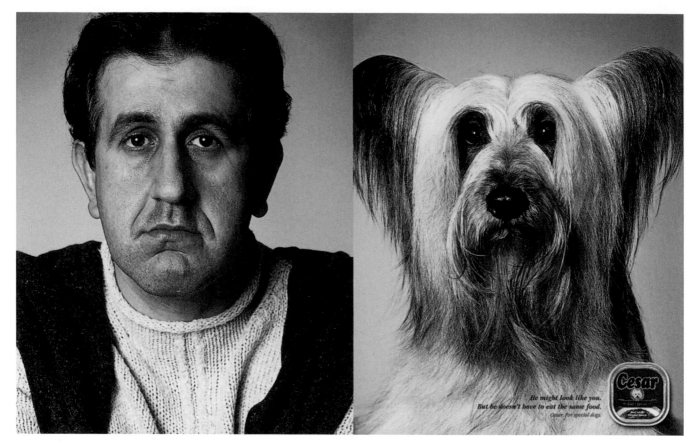

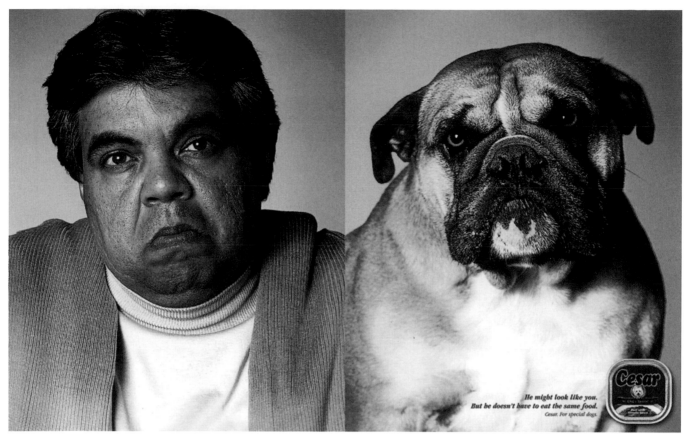

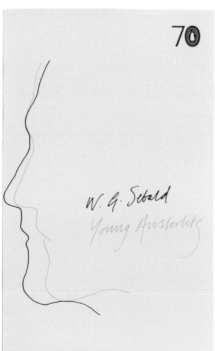

He might look like you.
But he doesn't have to eat the same food.
Cesar. For special dogs.

Dogs and Their Owners (above and opposite)
This witty 2007 campaign for Cesar dog food juxtaposes dogs with their owners. It brings a smile to the faces of viewers and sparks recognition that we all know someone who looks like their pet.

David Pearson, *Young Austerlitz* book cover (left)
This brilliantly simple book cover juxtaposes the profile of a young man's face with that of his much older self. In just two hand-drawn lines the designer David Pearson encapsulates the passage of a man's life from innocence to experience. *See* www.davidpearsondesign.com

DIY
Take viewers on exciting journeys by using juxtaposition.

Brainjack
Juxtaposition communicates because the brain instantly attempts to make a link between the things that are seen. The imagination fills in the journey from one image to another.

K

Knowledge

The greater your knowledge, the more sources of inspiration you can call upon. A message that engages a viewer's knowledge – in particular if that knowledge is hard come by – can make the recipient feel special, included and rewarded for their smartness. What do you know? Be porous to the world. Be porous to knowledge.

Stefanie Posavec and David McCandless, *Left vs. Right*, 2009
Posavec and McCandless condense world politics into a single provocative design in this project created for the book *Information is Beautiful* written by McCandless. Knowledge – information, facts and principles learned through time – is presented with incredible simplicity, clarity and structure.

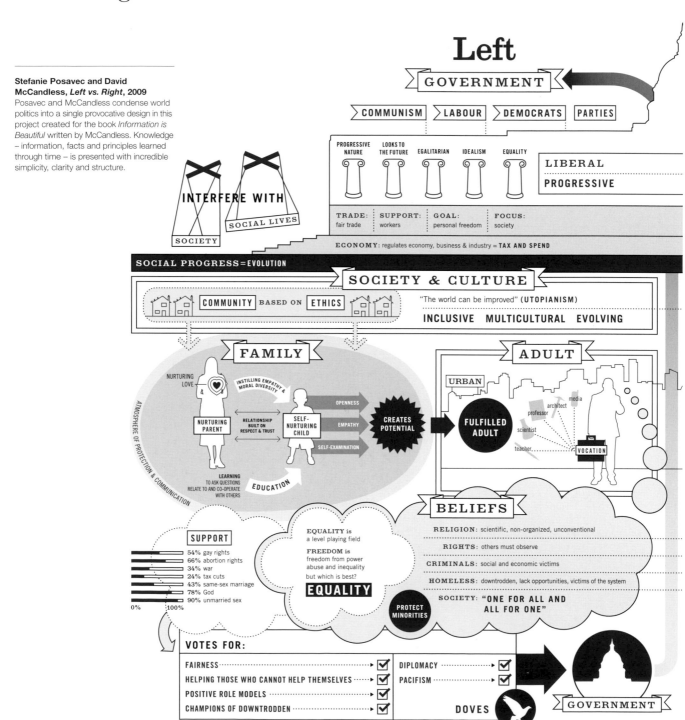

Left

GOVERNMENT

COMMUNISM | LABOUR | DEMOCRATS | PARTIES

PROGRESSIVE NATURE | LOOKS TO THE FUTURE | EGALITARIAN | IDEALISM | EQUALITY

LIBERAL
PROGRESSIVE

TRADE: fair trade | SUPPORT: workers | GOAL: personal freedom | FOCUS: society

ECONOMY: regulates economy, business & industry = **TAX AND SPEND**

SOCIAL PROGRESS = EVOLUTION

INTERFERE WITH SOCIAL LIVES
SOCIETY

SOCIETY & CULTURE

COMMUNITY BASED ON ETHICS

"The world can be improved" (UTOPIANISM)

INCLUSIVE MULTICULTURAL EVOLVING

FAMILY

NURTURING LOVE
INSTILLING EMPATHY & MORAL DIVERSITY

NURTURING PARENT
RELATIONSHIP BUILT ON RESPECT & TRUST
SELF-NURTURING CHILD

OPENNESS
EMPATHY
SELF-EXAMINATION

CREATES POTENTIAL

ATMOSPHERE OF PROTECTION & COMMUNICATION

LEARNING TO ASK QUESTIONS RELATE TO AND CO-OPERATE WITH OTHERS

EDUCATION

ADULT

URBAN

FULFILLED ADULT

media
architect
professor
scientist
teacher
VOCATION

BELIEFS

RELIGION: scientific, non-organized, unconventional

RIGHTS: others must observe

CRIMINALS: social and economic victims

HOMELESS: downtrodden, lack opportunities, victims of the system

SOCIETY: **"ONE FOR ALL AND ALL FOR ONE"**

SUPPORT
54% gay rights
66% abortion rights
34% war
24% tax cuts
43% same-sex marriage
78% God
90% unmarried sex
0%   100%

EQUALITY is a level playing field

FREEDOM is freedom from power abuse and inequality but which is best?

EQUALITY

PROTECT MINORITIES

VOTES FOR:

FAIRNESS ⋯⋯⋯⋯⋯⋯ ☑
HELPING THOSE WHO CANNOT HELP THEMSELVES ⋯⋯ ☑
POSITIVE ROLE MODELS ⋯⋯⋯⋯ ☑
CHAMPIONS OF DOWNTRODDEN ⋯⋯ ☑

DIPLOMACY ⋯⋯⋯ ☑
PACIFISM ⋯⋯⋯ ☑

DOVES

GOVERNMENT

'The unpremeditated, effortless spark of creativity does not arrive in an unprepared mind. It is the outcome of extensive learning and experience.'

Eugene Sadler-Smith, Professor of Management Development and Organizational Behaviour

'If you cease to stop wondering you cease to live.'

Einstein, theoretical physicist

'Every really good creative person in advertising whom I have ever met always had two characteristics. First, there was no subject he could not easily get interested in – from, say, Egyptian burial customs to modern art. Second, he was an extensive browser in all fields of information.'

James Webb Young, adman

'Man cannot have too much knowledge.'

Thomas Hardy, writer

Right

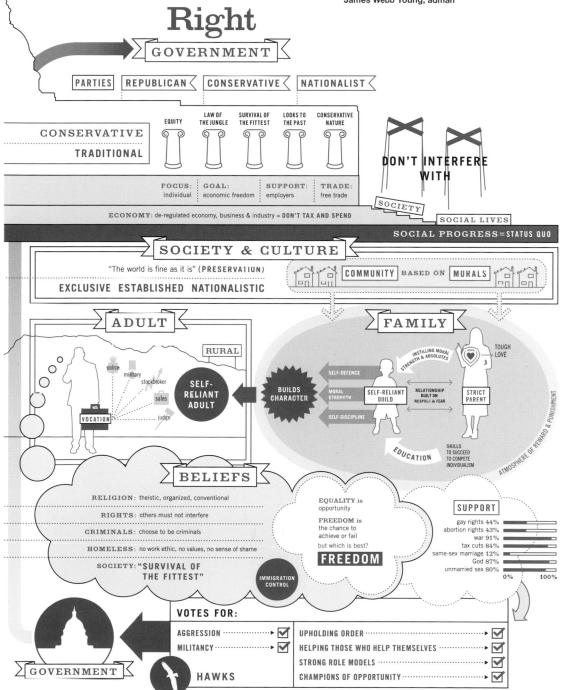

GOVERNMENT

PARTIES | REPUBLICAN | CONSERVATIVE | NATIONALIST

CONSERVATIVE
TRADITIONAL

EQUITY | LAW OF THE JUNGLE | SURVIVAL OF THE FITTEST | LOOKS TO THE PAST | CONSERVATIVE NATURE

FOCUS: individual | GOAL: economic freedom | SUPPORT: employers | TRADE: free trade

ECONOMY: de-regulated economy, business & industry = **DON'T TAX AND SPEND**

DON'T INTERFERE WITH

SOCIETY

SOCIAL LIVES

SOCIAL PROGRESS = STATUS QUO

SOCIETY & CULTURE

"The world is fine as it is" (PRESERVATION)

EXCLUSIVE ESTABLISHED NATIONALISTIC

COMMUNITY BASED ON MURALS

ADULT

RURAL

police / military / stockbroker / sales / judge

VOCATION

SELF-RELIANT ADULT

BUILDS CHARACTER

FAMILY

INSTILLING MORAL STRENGTH & ABSOLUTES

TOUGH LOVE

SELF-DEFENCE

MORAL STRENGTH

SELF-RELIANT CHILD

RELATIONSHIP BUILT ON RESPECT & FEAR

STRICT PARENT

SELF-DISCIPLINE

EDUCATION

SKILLS TO SUCCEED TO COMPETE INDIVIDUALISM

ATMOSPHERE OF REWARD & PUNISHMENT

BELIEFS

RELIGION: theistic, organized, conventional

RIGHTS: others must not interfere

CRIMINALS: choose to be criminals

HOMELESS: no work ethic, no values, no sense of shame

SOCIETY: "SURVIVAL OF THE FITTEST"

EQUALITY is opportunity

FREEDOM is the chance to achieve or fail but which is best?

FREEDOM

IMMIGRATION CONTROL

SUPPORT

gay rights 44%
abortion rights 43%
war 91%
tax cuts 84%
same-sex marriage 12%
God 87%
unmarried sex 80%

0% — 100%

VOTES FOR:

AGGRESSION ☑ | UPHOLDING ORDER ☑
MILITANCY ☑ | HELPING THOSE WHO HELP THEMSELVES ☑
| STRONG ROLE MODELS ☑
| CHAMPIONS OF OPPORTUNITY ☑

GOVERNMENT

HAWKS

L

Laughter

Can you put a smile on someone's face? Better still, can you make them laugh out loud? Laughter brings great pleasure and at its best it can be euphoric. It is so powerful a human response that we can do ourselves damage by attempting to contain and suppress it; we can giggle and laugh long before we can talk. Writer and comedian Charlie Brooker described the effect of a great joke: 'It rapidly expands in their head like an instant inflatable dinghy, tickles their comprehension and surprise cells simultaneously, and bingo: out pops a laugh.'

No Wind (right)
Our knowledge that icon Marilyn's skirt should be boisterously billowing coupled with the information that the ad is for an anti-flatulence product makes this poster laugh-out-loud funny. It was created by agency Ogilvy & Mather. *See* Icons, Movies.

Club 18–30 (opposite top)
British Holiday firm Club 18–30 are the butt of numerous stand-up comedians' jokes for their cheap package holidays for young people. This great 1992 ad created by Saatchi & Saatchi is packed with visual jokes that wonderfully play up to their reputation for providing holidays offering plentiful opportunities for pleasure-seeking with the opposite sex.

Pirelli Bus (opposite below)
Alan Fletcher, Colin Forbes and Bob Gill created this great visual joke in which passengers on the top deck of the bus complete the figures wearing Pirelli slippers. The campaign is from 1962 – predating by a nearly half a century other highly creative uses of public transport vehicles to spread messages. *See* New venues for messages.

Art jokes
American artist Richard Prince collects jokes. He stencils series of them on to large canvases in black paint, re-creating the rapid-fire delivery of a stand-up comic. One series reads: I KNEW A GUY WHO WAS SO RICH HE COULD SKI UP HILL. ANOTHER ONE. I TOLD MY MOTHER-IN-LAW MY HOUSE WAS HER HOUSE, LAST WEEK SHE SOLD IT. ANOTHER ONE.

Roy Lichtenstein's paintings of enlarged brush strokes and his huge painting of the word ART are great art jokes, as are Andy Warhol's series of painting-by-numbers and dollar sign paintings. Jeff Koon's enormous kitsch sculptures are also very, very funny. *See* So bad it's good.

ACTAL **PLUS**
ANTI-FLATULENT ANTACID

NO WIND.

Comic communication

Comedians generally create laughter with a preamble that leads the audience in a particular direction. Their minds race ahead to where they think it is leading and are suddenly jerked back with an unexpected twist they don't see coming. Comic messages conclude with a punch line that can hit home like an unexpected blow from a boxer. Jokes are verbally dextrous, poetry for everyman. A critic described comedian Jimmy Carr's one-liners as having the formal perfection of a haiku – a precisely constructed Japanese poem (*see* Maths).

Jokes can be told about anything – provided they are told in the right way. Nothing is sacred in great comedy, and they can break taboos and be transgressive, crossing lines that only they can cross. Jokes can show us the bars that imprison us, and laughter can temporarily set us free by mocking our entrapment.

DIY
Harness what makes you laugh. Look back on your experiences. Making a joke based on a real experience can lead to an honesty that rings true and connects directly with a viewer. *See* Satire.

Brainjack
Laughter is a reflex response. It is involuntary and unstoppable, like a knee jerk, and as a result it is an unstoppable means of communication that can override any defence.

Observational comedy
Watch, listen and look. Tap into what makes people laugh. Know all the comedy greats from the music hall, silent comedy, television and the movies. Examine the construction and delivery of comic messages. Collect jokes and examine the use of words and economy of delivery.

Physical comedy
Be inspired by slapstick. It provokes laughter through fast, farcical, highly physical comedy rather than the use of language. In slapstick the human body is oblivious to harm when it falls from high buildings or is run over. The 'little guy' is often the hero, who reassuringly defeats those who are too big for their boots.

Cartoon comedy
Examine the visual language of cartoon strips and see how ideas are delivered in a sequence of images. Television cartoons also burst with ideas in the way they use images and sound. An example is the wonderful convention that a number of circling tweeting birds moving around a character's head signifies he has suffered a bump to the head.

Making faces

Faces are fascinating. We are drawn instinctively to images of faces and instantly recognize their expressions. Smiling life-size ones attract us to the covers of magazines, crying ones make us sad, and screaming ones are arresting and shocking. The simplest representation of eyes and a mouth can create a face with an individual personality.

Salvador Dalí, *Face of Mae West (can be used as Surrealist apartment)*, 1934. Dalí recreates the face of movie icon Mae West in a design for an interior in which her lips are the sofa, her nose a sideboard and her hair the curtains. The lips sofa later went into production and the room has been constructed in the Dalí museum in Figueres in Catalonia, Spain – when standing at a certain point in the room the face suddenly coalesces. *See* Icons, Illusion, One thing looks like another.

'The face is the first thing we know, our mother's faces are the first landscape we learn and images of the face work brilliantly at any scale – tiny or massive.'

Sally Potter, film director

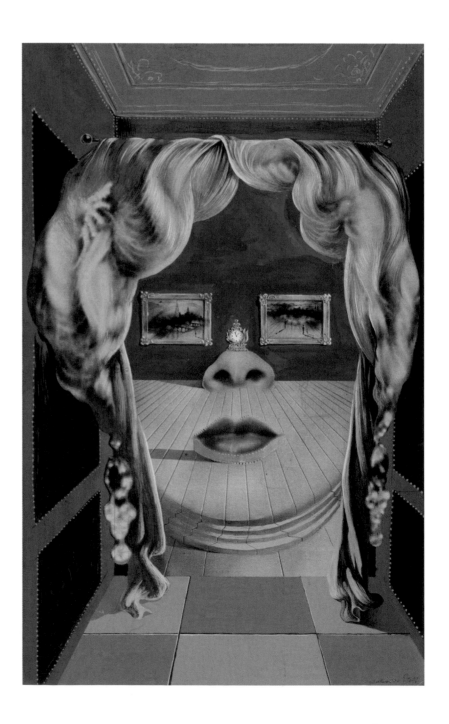

Finding faces

The fact that cars have faces created by their headlights and radiator grille and some buildings have faces made by windows and doors has been used as a source of ideas in many movies and cartoons, and in illustration, design and advertising.

The design group Pentagram created a famous collection of photographs of faces found in the shapes of door handles, corkscrews and pencil sharpners.

Designer Tibor Kalman created another collection for *Colors* magazine (*see* overleaf).

Barney Bubbles, *I Love the Sound of Breaking Glass*, record single cover, 1978 (below left)
Barney Bubbles – aka Colin Fulcher – a brilliant designer principally for the UK music industry, frequently assembled faces for unlikely elements in his graphic work. He worked with hippy bands and on psychedelic magazines in the 1960s before designing for the pub rock and punk scene in the 1970s.

Children's Album (below right)
Instruments used to create the songs on Glen Gordon's CD for children make a winking face. Design by Dave Farrow, 1994.

Magazine features (bottom left)
Illustration by Jimmy Turrell for an article in *The Observer* magazine facing up to the dangers inherent in becoming a music journalist. See www.jimmyturrell.com

Vince Frost, *Type Primer*, book cover (bottom right)
A type face created by Vince Frost for a book on the principles of typography. *See* www.frostdesign.com.au

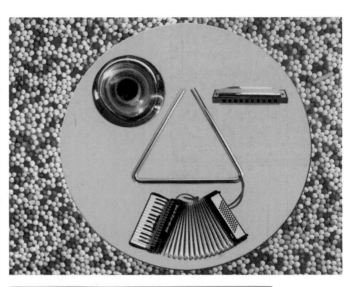

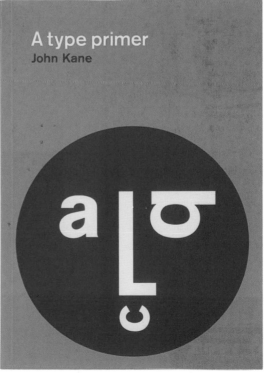

Faces from *Colors* magazine (below)
A huge range of expressions are seen in this collection of faces photographed in the streets – from a 1996 issue of *Colors* magazine designed by Hungarian-born designer Tibor Kalman.

Intercom face (bottom left)
The bells, nameplates and intercom grille provide a startling welcome at this Venetian apartment.

Metal plates (bottom right)
Unscrewed-up faces.

Nick Hornby *Otherwise Pandemonium* book cover (opposite)
Designer Jamie Keenan made a face when briefed to create this book cover. *See* www.keenandesign.com

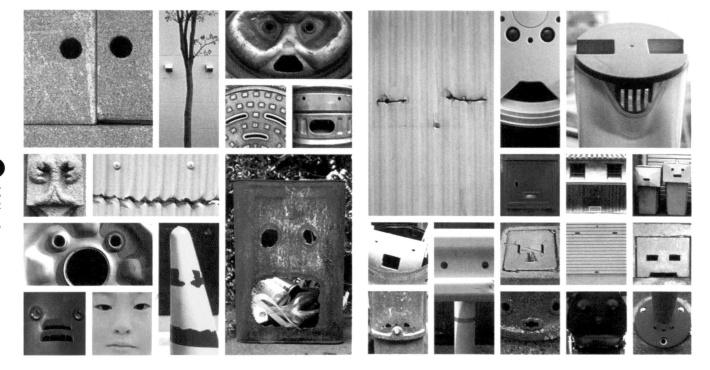

Making faces

M

Videocassette

NICK HORNBY

OTHERWISE PANDEMONIUM

M

Making faces

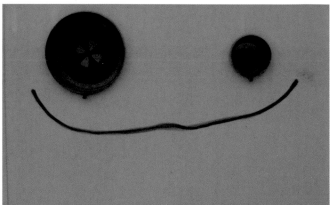

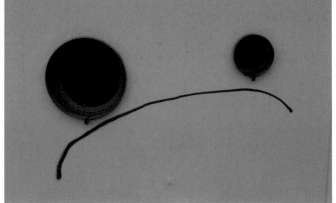

Face saving (this page and opposite)
Some of the author's collection of faces
spotted on his travels. *See* Finding
ideas, Travel.

DIY
Make faces!

Brainjack
The arrangement of the elements
that make the face create a
character who speaks to the
viewer. The idea is delivered
through the relationship formed
between the elements and the
expression on the face.

Making maps

The shapes of the world's nations are instantly recognizable; we have learnt them from geography lessons, atlases and the maps on classroom walls. We all know Italy is boot-shaped and is kicking Sicily into the Mediterranean.

Cartographers, designers of maps, have developed an easily understood language of colours, contours and symbols to represent information such as borders, navigation routes and the heights of mountains. Maps can additionally convey invisible concepts like wealth and political or religious allegiances in clear, simple ways. These conventions of maps and map-making are a rich source of inspiration for creative people, and designers and artists have delighted in playing with them to deliver a variety of messages about the world.

Kathy Prendergast, *Between Love and Paradise*, **2002**
Irish artist Kathy Prendergast creates maps using real place names that relate to human feelings, experiences and emotions – in this map you can discover rapture and love as well as finding confidence. Prendergast writes: 'For the last few years I have been researching place-names with the idea of producing an "Emotional Atlas of the World."'
See www.kerlin.ie

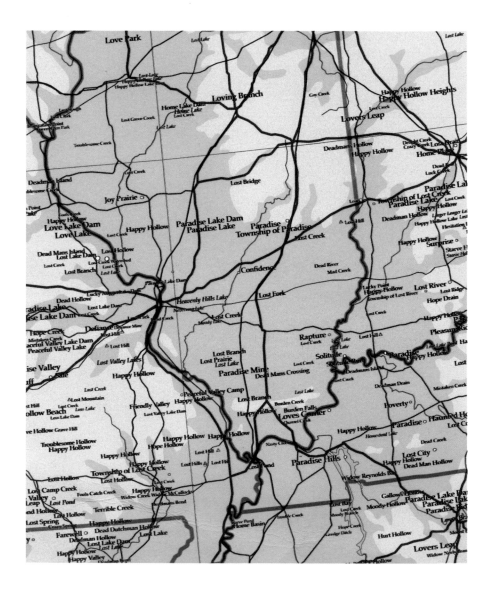

Maps of the imagination

People have made maps of realms beyond the known world, such as heaven and hell. Artists have also created personal ones that allow viewers to navigate through their heroes and inspirations, happiness and misery, love and marriage. One designer even attempted to chart the road to success.

Africa book cover (below left)
Designer Alistair Hall created this striking book cover boldly cropping the photo into the shape of Africa. Photography by Patti Gower. *See* www.wemadethis.co.uk

South America poster (below middle)
Art students Dan Hirst and James Crickmore created this poster entitled *Meat, No Veg*. It highlights that South America is now largely focused on supplying the world with meat, the size of the sprig of parsley reflects what is left of the Amazon rainforest while the faint green patch shows the area it once covered.

The Art Atlas, book cover (below right)
This book cover maps out the book's content – how physical and political geography has shaped the world's art. Designed in 2008 by Studio8 Design.

Chinese propaganda poster (bottom left)
A contemporary Chinese propaganda poster celebrating the nation's unity and ethnic diversity, even the most densely industrialized areas are portrayed as blooming with flowers.

Camouflage world map (bottom right)
The world is concealed by military camouflage in this art student's poster from February 2003. It aimed to make viewers think about the possible consequences of the invasion of Iraq.

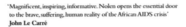

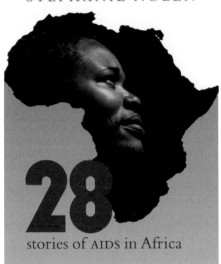

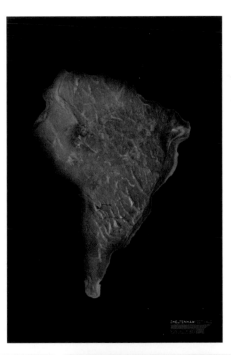

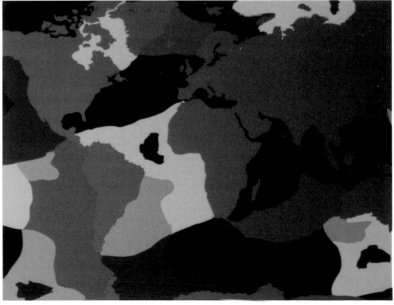

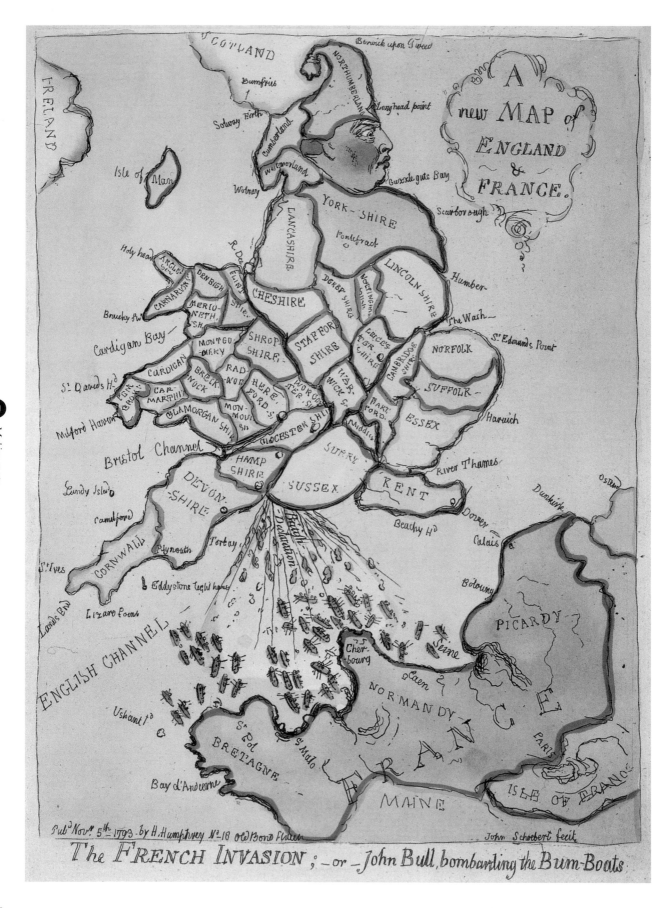

James Gillray, *A New Map of England and France*, *The French Invasion*, or, *John Bull Bombarding the Bum-Boats*, 1793 (opposite)
King George III evacuates his bowels into the face of France with such force that the fleets of invading French boats are dispersed. Gillray's brilliant drawing transforms the map of England into the defecating king and the coastline of France into a profile of a face. *See* Caricature, One Thing Looks Like Another.

Crime Uncovered Map of Britain, magazine cover (below left)
Shattered reinforced glass makes a map of Britain in this powerful and superbly executed cover created for the *Observer Magazine's* 2003 crime special.

johnson banks, *London Republik* (below centre)
Designers Michael Johnson, Julia Woollams and Kath Tudball created this poster for London listings magazine *Time Out* for a special edition about a 'republic of London'

– 'we decided to show London as the best bit of the UK'. *See* www.johnsonbanks.co.uk

Ruth Adams, British Milk campaign (below right)
A 2007 ad shot by photographer Ruth Adams highlighting the benefits of drinking milk. *See* www.ruthadams.co.uk

John Sorrell, *Creative Island II*, book cover design, 2008 (bottom left)
Sorrell's book features designers, architecture, engineering, furniture, fashion, jewellery, and

graphics that have shaped Britain.

Jimmy Turrell, Map of Britain (bottom right)
Map designed for the *Guardian* newspaper by Jimmy Turrell for a feature on events taking place in Britain over the Christmas period. 'There were originally loads of logos all over it but when I removed them I thought it was stronger – almost like different bits of Christmas wrapping paper,' said Turrell. *See* www.jimmyturrell.com

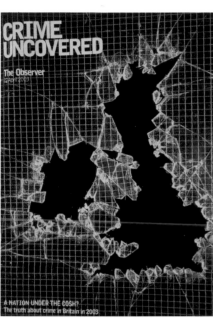

DIY
Geographic maps with precise, flat plan depictions of the world offer by far the quickest way to represent a country or continent. Viewers' familiarity with their outlines means creative images that use these maps can be greatly stretched and distorted but what inspired them remains instantly recognizable.

Be inspired by maps and mapping, explore maps and atlases. Using their conventions creatively can provide alternative views of our lives as well as the world.

Brainjack
Geographic maps are shapes that are known and trusted; a viewer's knowledge and mental picture of a shape as it should be can contrast memorably with the way it has been manipulated.

Materials

Materials are inspirational. Our first creative materials were things that were to hand – flint, stone and wood; later we learnt to use glass, silver and gold. Every material has inherent natural qualities, strengths and beauty. Experiment with as many materials as you can. See Garage genius.

Marc Quinn, *Self*, 2009
Quinn's creative material comes from his body. *Self* is one of a series of self-portraits created by the artist using ten pints of his own blood, frozen inside a cast of his head. The blood is removed by his doctor a pint at a time, every six weeks. Quinn plans to make a new version every five years to record his ageing.

Building materials – a palette of bricks

The history of Western creativity changed in the mid-1970s when artist Carl Andre exhibited 120 building bricks arranged in a rectangle at the Tate Gallery in London. Until then art had traditionally been made with precious or expensive materials. Newspapers took it upon themselves to protest on behalf of the public; they denounced the bricks as 'not art' and claimed that 'a kid could do better than that'. The installation, now known simply as 'the Tate bricks', changed the palette of possible creative materials forever.

Materials from the natural world

Natural materials can be used in original ways. Artist Richard Wilson created an unforgettable installation with oil (*see* overleaf): viewers entered it via a walled walkway and found themselves surrounded, waste deep, with oceans of black oil that totally filled the gallery. Critic Waldemar Januszczak wrote that, 'the presence of this much oil pressing in on you from all sides made your body instinctively nervous. What if the walls gave way? It felt dangerous and claustrophobic. This combination of danger and beauty is what made the piece unforgettable.'

Damien Hirst uses butterflies, cows, calves and living flies, while Banksy featured live rats in a memorable installation. Brazilian artist Vik Muniz used earth as his material and mechanical diggers as his tools; he carved huge shapes into the ground in South America and photographed them from above. The shapes included gigantic 'paper' planes, plug sockets and umbrellas (*see* Rescaling). Muniz also experimented with chocolate as a drawing material and used a crop-dusting plane to draw cartoonish cloud shapes in cloudless blue skies above New York.

Man-made materials

The Chinese designer Cai Guo-Chang uses fireworks as creative materials. He created the unforgettable opening ceremony for the Beijing Olympics in 2008, when giant's footsteps made of exploding rockets paced across the city towards the Olympic stadium, symbolizing the march of history. *See* Symbols.

Material from man

Materials from the human body have inspired creative works: the British artist Marc Quinn produced a startling self-portrait using 10 pints (5.7 litres) of his own blood (*see* opposite).

Man as material

The human body has always inspired creative people. Artists and photographers have created work that looks at its textures and contours, its strengths, frailties and beauty, its grace and distortion in motion and how it changes as it ages. Photographer Spencer Tunick uses tens of thousands of naked volunteers as his creative material, and poses them for photographs in famous locations around the world.

New uses for old materials

The reuse of old materials for new purposes has been described as upcycling. Low-status, rejected and unfashionable items can be combined, overprinted or enlivened – for example, old china plates can be refired with new designs. Ron Arad created his famous Rover chair after upcycling a car seat found in a London scrapyard (*see* overleaf).

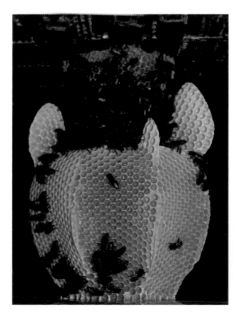

Tomas Gabzdil Libertiny, *Made by Bees*
This wonderful honeycomb vase was created in 2007 by Slovak designer Tomas Gabzdil Libertiny with the help of tens of thousands bees. He wrote 'I made a series of vases from beeswax before trying to push it further by asking whether a vase could be made where the material is born, thus in a beehive.' The unique shape was made over the course of days as the bees added their honeycomb around wax shaped by Libertiny.

Ron Arad, *Concrete Stereo*, 1983 (far left)
Arad used materials and techniques from the construction industry to create this brutal but beautiful music system embedding turntable, amplifier and speakers in concrete poured into wire frames. He poured the concrete roughly and left gaps to reveal the reinforcing wires preferring the resultant post-apocalyptic look to a more polished finish.

Dan Knight, *Mother Mary*, 1999 (left)
Knight gives new life to things that have been thrown away. Garish discarded cards, used by London prostitutes to advertise their services, are the material for this sculpture.

Container City, Trinity Buoy Wharf, London, 2003 (bottom left)
Urban Space Management speedily rejuvenate derelict city land by upcyling old shipping containers. They smartly spotted the possibilities of the steel boxes as the perfect material to create low-cost art and design studios – the containers being cheap to buy, easy to renovate, quick to stack and not requiring traditional foundations.

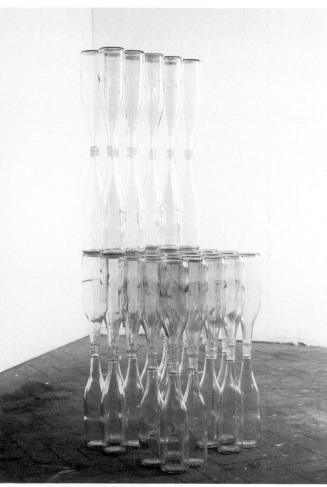

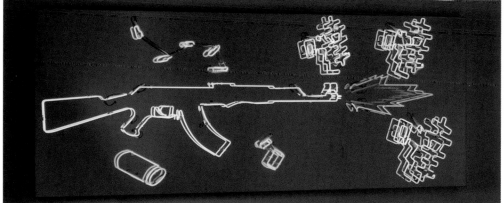

Richard Wilson, *20:50*, 1987 (opposite centre right)
The spellbinding oil room in the Saatchi Gallery in London uses sump oil as its creative material. *See* Mirror, mirror.

Steve Messam, *Souvenir*, 2006 (opposite bottom right)
British artist Messam used dozens of umbrellas bought at a tourist gift shop as his creative material to build this installation.

Ron Arad, *The Rover Chair*, 1981 (top left)
Arad remounted a car seat found in a scrap yard on inexpensive modular tubing, brilliantly fusing old and new materials to create a beautiful chair. *See* Fusion.

Dan Knight, *Invisible Chair*, 2004 (top right)
Artist Dan Knight created this wonderful chair combining bottles to create both structural strength and beautiful shapes.

Island 6, *To be or not to be*, neon, 2009
Neon tubing is a material traditionally used in advertising displays, here art collective Island6 use it to recreate a global symbol of bloodshed, conflict and violence – the AK47 machine gun. *See* Symbols.

 DIY
Explore conventional and unconventional materials. Try to see the ones that are available to you in a new light and find new qualities and possibilities in them. Play to the strengths of a material. Discover how far you can push it.

Visiting hardware stores, builders' yards and factories can lead to the discovery of inspiring new materials and production techniques. On a factory visit Arad chanced across a technique for inflating heated aluminium through steel stencils, which led to the design and production of innovative tables and vases.

 Brainjack
Materials can make viewers think again. An idea that is realized with an unexpected material or built by finding a new use for an old one can delight and surprise. Seeing a material in a new light makes the viewer re-evaluate its worth.

M

Materials

113

Maths

M.C. Escher, *Smaller and Smaller*, 1943
Dutch graphic artist Escher's amazing
drawing of lizards was inspired by seeing
tessellated tiles.

*Fans of Pythagoras believe everything in the universe comes
from, and can be explained by, maths. The sixth-century
BC mathematician, scientist, astronomer and philosopher
wrote that 'number is the ruler of forms and ideas'. There
is huge creativity in mathematics. It has its own unique
patterns, rhythms and shapes, and can be elegant
and beautiful.*

Do the maths

Writer and professor Marcus du Sautoy described finding inspiration in mathematics as being like entering a secret garden: 'in that garden I discovered that mathematics also has great stories. Unsolved mysteries like the enigma of prime numbers. Magical mathematical machines that could help you see in four dimensions' and 'mathematicians who journeyed to infinity and beyond.'

Tessellations

Mathematical concepts inspired Maurits Cornelis Escher. When he visited the Alhambra in Granada, Spain, he became fascinated by the geometric arrangements of square, triangular and hexagonal tiles that fit together in the perfect patterns known as tessellations. He called them 'the richest source of inspiration that I have ever tapped'. Escher created extraordinary images based on tessellations and was further inspired by other mathematical concepts and ideas. His brilliant work includes attempts to visualize infinity (see opposite).

Tessellation also inspired the English designer William Morris; and maths and architecture = the Pentagon building.

To infinity and beyond

Multidisciplinary designer Ross Cooper was inspired by Escher when he created a music promo for the band Wild Beasts (see overleaf). He recalls: 'Our inspiration came from a lithograph created by Escher in 1954, called the *Print Room*. It's based on a mathematical technique he created and shows a man standing in a gallery looking at a picture which spirals round until you can see the man again. The middle is blank, which Escher has signed in the centre. He'd been unable to finish the centre because it was too complicated. Dutch computer programmers had figured out how to write the software to create the effect with still photographs and complete the image in a way that Escher was unable to do. The formula had become publicly available and we pushed this further by doing it with moving images – though it was so complicated we had to borrow ten computers from all our friends to make it work.'

Musical maths

Mathematics has inspired musicians as well as artists, designers and writers. It is closely related to music with numbers playing an important part in the performance, writing and language of music; for example, in two-four time, octaves, treble clefs and fifths, sevenths, ninths and elevenths.

Du Sautoy wrote that, 'There are so many interesting themes that can be investigated: Ghanaian and Indian rhythms exploit the indivisibility of the primes; the tension between fractions and irrational numbers like the square root of two'; and that 'modern music by Schoenberg and Messiaen is a musical expression of the mathematics of symmetry.'

Golden numbers

The musician Vijay Iyer uses mathematical ideas when he composes: 'They help me find sounds and rhythms that I might never have made otherwise.' Iyer examined the work of the thirteenth-century Italian mathematician Fibonacci who gave his name to the set of numbers that begins 1, 1, 2, 3, 5, 8, 13, 21, 34, 55, 89. Each successive number in the sequence is created by adding the previous two together. The ratio between successive numbers as the sequence continues to evolve is …1.6, 1.625, 1.615, 1.619… Iyer observed: 'As you go up the sequence, this ratio gets closer and closer to the famous irrational number called the "Golden Ratio": 1.6180339887. This ratio has been observed frequently in dimensional proportions across many different contexts – in architecture from the Pyramids of Giza and the Parthenon, to constructions by Le Corbusier and Mies van der Rohe; images by artists from Da Vinci and Albrecht Dürer to Juan Gris, Mondrian and Dalí; and rhythmic durations and pitch ratios in works by composers from Bartók and Debussy to John Coltrane.' The golden ratio is believed to create a harmonious and pleasing aesthetic, and occurs in the natural world – for example, in some leaf patterns and the arrangement of pine cones.

Maths and creative writing

Mathematics permeates creative writing. Shakespeare wrote in pentameters, where each line is made up of five units of rhythm. This is the common metre of poetry written in English. Japanese poetry features the haiku which follows a strict mathematical form that uses 17 syllables in three unrhymed lines of five, seven and five syllables.

Maths and digitality

Without mathematics there would be no digital photography, digital images, music downloads or any form of creativity made or distributed by computers. Every piece of digital information is recorded as a digit or number. It is these numbers collectively that allow digital information to be stored, transmitted and reformed. See Digitality.

Digital variations

Iraqi-born teacher and artist Mowfak Gowley created a digital artwork, *Random Mondrian*, in which he programmed a computer to generate infinite variations of Mondrian's compositions.

Escher inspired
Stills from a promotional video created by
multidisciplinary artist Ross Cooper inspired
by the work of E. C. Esher.

Geometric Chinese paving (above left)
Repeating geometric patterns make up the path of a public garden in Suzhou, China

Alhambra tiling (left and above)
Two examples of the numerous variations of Islamic tiling that can be seen at the Alhambra Palace in Granada, Spain. Mesmerizing and incredibly beautiful, some date from the fourteenth century.

 DIY
Explore the magic of numbers as a source of inspiration. Discover the work of inspiring mathletes including Pythagoras, Fibonacci and Brahmagupta.

 Brainjack
Mathematics makes patterns that the brain finds naturally appealing.

Mirror, mirror

Mirrors create compelling reflections and distortions. They are integral to our daily lives – we have intimate relationships with them each day in our private preparations before going out to face the world. Images of people gazing into mirrors can symbolize vanity and narcissism (excessive self-interest, called after Narcissus, a beautiful youth who became rapt and trapped by his own reflection). See Symbols.

Island6, *Mirror*
As viewers gaze into this antique wooden mirror a decidedly unexpected reflection suddenly appears on its scratched surface – that of a beautiful young Chinese woman carefully applying her make-up, she continues until the viewer departs. It was created by art collective Liu Dao who wrote 'Chinese culture has undergone a great change in the last decade, we wanted to reflect the tension between old and new, a tension between tradition and the newest technology of which China is the cradle.' *See* www.island6.org

Mirrored mercury
Alexander Calder created his unforgettable *Mercury Fountain* in 1937 designed as a memorial to Republican soldiers killed in the Spanish Civil War. It brilliantly uses the mirroring quality of the metallic liquid, which flows endlessly across curved terraces to create mesmerizing, ever-changing reflections and distortions of its surroundings. It is sited at the Miró Museum in Barcelona. *See* Materials.

Sound mirrors
Huge, concave concrete structures were built along the south coast of Britain before the Second World War. Known as 'sound mirrors', they provided warning of possible invasions by greatly amplifying distant noises. They now look like crumbling distant relatives of Anish Kapoor's massive mirrors.

House of mirrors

A visit to a house of mirrors at a fairground or at the seaside provides us with the joyous experience of seeing our bodies instantly squeezed or bloated. Mumbai-born artist Anish Kapoor takes the experience into art galleries and public squares with his vast mirror sculptures. His work takes distortions to extremes with huge concave and convex shapes; he even creates massive three-dimensional sculptures with mirrored surfaces (*see* Rescaling). His masterpiece is *Cloud Gate*, a mammoth tear-shaped sculpture in Millennium Park in Chicago, which is so big that visitors can walk under its surface.

Mirror, mirror, mirror, mirror

As well as having the capacity to distort, mirrors can be combined to create visions of infinity. This has inspired numerous creative people, including photographer William Klein in his dynamic fashion story *Antonia Mirrors*

and film director Joseph Mankiewicz in the dramatic finale of his film *All About Eve*.

Digital mirrors

Artists have been inspired to fuse the characteristics of mirrors with digital technology. Chinese art collective Liu Dao created a series of installations using old-fashioned mirrors found in junk shops in which the reflective surface on the reverse of the mirrors had been subtly scratched and sandwiched with computer screens. As viewers look at their reflections other faces suddenly loom out of the mirror towards them (*see* opposite). Jerusalem-born Daniel Rozin created a digital *Weave Mirror* (*see* below) that activates as someone approaches. A rotating warp and weft of graded cylinders spins into action and re-creates an impression of the viewer and their movements. In another brilliant installation he created a similar effect with a huge grid of large, moving, shiny balls. *See* Digitality.

Daniel Rozin, *Weave Mirror* (above)
Rozin's mirror is a wonderful whirring, spinning Heath-Robinsonesque contraption. The artist has created many installations and sculptures using mirrors.

Mirrored illy cup (above)
Neil Aitken and Ross Cooper created this mirrored cup for illy in 2000. Espresso drinkers found the reflection of a seemingly abstract pattern on the saucer revealed the coffee producer's logo. A wonderful 'reverse' idea – as mirrors are known for distorting images not unifying them. *See* Reverse.

Hugh Hales-Tooke, Paul Smith ad (left)
Photographer Hales-Tooke cleverly uses a mirror and models to simultaneously show the front and back view of a suit in this witty fashion shot – recalling surrealist artist René Magritte's painting *Not To Be Reproduced*. *See* www.hughhales-tooke.com

DIY
Use mirrors to distort and reflect the world.

Brainjack
Mirrors and other reflective surfaces are frequently used in graphic design, illustration and advertising to reveal an alternative view of a subject. Viewers are engaged because their mental expectation of a symmetrical reflection is confounded and an unexpected comparison is made. Ideas delivered in this way can impact with great simplicity and power.

Movies

M

Movies

Must-see movies for creative people
A Bout De Souffle, Barbarella, Battleship Potemkin, (Cocteau's) La Belle et La Bête, Blade Runner, Blue Velvet, Brazil, Cabaret, The Cabinet of Dr Caligari, Citizen Kane, La Dolce Vita, Duck Soup, The General, Gold Diggers of 1933, La Jetée, Kind Hearts and Coronets, A Matter of Life and Death, Night of the Hunter, Pan's Labyrinth, Psycho, Pulp Fiction, Ran, Sunset Boulevard, The Tin Drum, 2001: A Space Odyssey, The Weeping Meadow, The Wizard of Oz.

Gregory Crewdson, *Untitled (Dream House Portfolio)*
Inspired by the look of the Spielberg movie *Close Encounters of The Third Kind* and films by David Lynch, artist Crewdson constructs dramatic, epic, haunting photographs. Directing a large crew to produce each photo – closing entire neighbourhoods for his shoots, using set builders, lighting directors, smoke, wind and rain machines – he carefully builds each image, which costs the same as a small movie to produce, he even casts Hollywood actors to star in his pictures.

Popular movies are highly influential and are universal reference points. Most people have seen, and many can quote lines from, Star Wars, The Terminator, The Wizard of Oz, Jaws *and the James Bond movies. Thanks to Walt Disney's* Pinocchio *we know that a liar's nose grows longer with each lie that is told, and because of Steven Spielberg's* ET *trick or treating has become a Halloween ritual in the United Kingdom.*

The public's knowledge of movies and the deep affection in which many are held means they have frequently been used as a source of ideas for advertising campaigns. Scenes from The Matrix, 2001: A Space Odyssey, Battleship Potemkin, Gladiator, The Great Escape, Godzilla, Oliver, Psycho, Ghostbusters, The Shining, Butch Cassidy and the Sundance Kid, The Deer Hunter *and* Bullet *have all been the basis for recent advertisements. Movie scenes are frequently parodied in television comedies and other films.*

Directors as inspiration

Be inspired by the way in which different directors tell stories and how ideas are communicated. Watch how the camera is positioned and moved, and how shots are framed. Learn from the ways in which directors edit and condense time to indicate that minutes, hours, days or even years have passed. Be inspired by magical movie sets and the colour and lighting used to create mood.

Movies and fashion

Many movies and movie stars have been influential in fashion design. For example, the outfits created by Edith Head that Grace Kelly and Tippi Hedren wore in their films for Alfred Hitchcock have inspired numerous designers, including John Galliano and Alexander McQueen.

Movies, in particular films centered on youth culture, have inspired and spread fashion crazes – *Quadrophenia* sparked the revival of the Mod look.

Movie soundtracks

Be inspired by how images are fused with music and sound in movies. Directors often create discordant juxtapositions, such as violent scenes set against contradictory soundtracks – the gang assaults in *A Clockwork Orange* are accompanied by 'Singing in the Rain'. *Reservoir Dogs* uses a similar combination of extreme brutality and upbeat music.

Silent movies

Be inspired by early silent movies which experimented with the newly discovered medium of film in inventive and creative ways. *See* Laughter.

Great movie scenes

The phrase 'a Busby Berkeley scene' has entered the English language as meaning a brilliant musical dance number. During the 1930s Berkeley specialized in directing dance scenes interspersed with scenes from movies by other directors. His masterpiece is *Gold Diggers of 1933*. One spectacular sequence not only features overhead shots of hundreds of dancers creating pulsating patterns; it also telescopes the entire history of the First World War and the Depression into a few minutes.

Alfred Hitchcock's visual trickery, invention and experimentation are extraordinarily inspiring. In a black-and-white movie red blood spurts on to the screen during a murder. In *Psycho,* 70 rapid shots show the brief shower-scene slaying, while all of *Rope* is shot in only eight takes, each of which lasts about 10 minutes during which the camera appears to move from room to room passing through solid walls. This was achieved by unseen stagehands who moved walls, props and furniture during the scenes.

Hallo Dalí!

Be inspired by artists and photographers who make movies. Artists Salvador Dalí, Jean Cocteau, Kenneth Anger and Derek Jarman, and photographers Bruce Weber, William Klein and Robert Frank, created films that use radically different aesthetics and storytelling techniques to those of the mainstream.

Be inspired by video directors who have become movie-makers; examples are Michel Gondry and Chris Cunningham.

Say hallo to Bollywood

Seek inspiration in movies from all over the world: from India, Japan, China, Russia, Korea and Iran. Get to know the 'world cinema' shelf in your local DVD store. India's colourful fantasy dance films, known as Bollywood movies, have inspired photographers Tim Walker, and Pierre et Gilles.

Movie stills and posters

Stills from movies often show the high points of a drama and are a powerful source of inspiration. Many fashion photographers have created stories based on them, and they inspired the early work of artist Cindy Sherman. Fashion designer Paul Smith produced a catalogue based on stills from *The Graduate*. Artist Francis Bacon used ones from *Battleship Potemkin* in his paintings, in particular an image of a nurse's tormented face from the Odessa Steps sequence. He used this as inspiration for more than 40 paintings of screaming popes.

We frequently remember films through still images, some of which become iconic. We know them from posters seen at cinemas, DVD covers and poster reproductions made to be Blu-Tacked or pinned to bedroom walls. Repeated viewing has imprinted the images on our minds. Some films use movie posters to help establish character: in *Saturday Night Fever* John Travolta has posters from *Rocky*, and of TV and film star Farah Fawcett, on the wall of his room.

Great title sequences

Title sequences are mini movies in themselves. Study their economy, how they evoke the movie and their use of typography. Masters of title design include Robert Brownjohn and Saul Bass. Bass pioneered the smart use of graffiti half a century ago in the titles for *West Side Story*. Some of his sequences stick in mind far longer than the films his work introduced. See also Kyle Cooper's great titles for *Seven*.

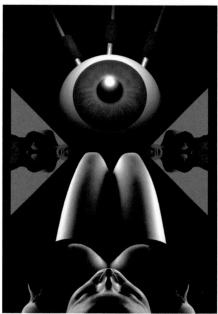

Clockwork Orange fashion
A series of fashion photos by David
Abrahams inspired by Stanley Kubrick's
movie *A Clockwork Orange*.
See www.davidabrahams.co.uk

Gavin Bond, *Cave Woman* **(far left)/** *The Outlaw* **(below)**
Photographer Gavin Bond often uses movies as a source of inspiration in his photographs of young American stars – for example photographing Johnny Knoxville and the other *Jackass* stars as the Three Stooges for *Vanity Fair* magazine. Here he recreates famous stills of Raquel Welch from the movie *One Million Years B.C.* (far left) and Jane Russell from *The Outlaw* (left below). *See* www.gavinbond.com

American Beauty ad (left)
A scene from the movie *American Beauty* inspired this campaign encouraging young people to use condoms. It was created by photographer Leah Evans.

DIY
Compile the movie scenes that connect to your project or brief. There are well-known scenes for almost every topic. How many of the following can you picture in your mind?

Famous scenes about eating. Famous scenes about drinking. Famous scenes about receiving a life-changing letter that offers a place at college or university. Famous scenes involving cars, taxis, coffee, hotels, cameras, haircuts and barbers, phones, shoes, book stores, guitars, jogging, bunk beds. Famous scenes about good and bad teachers.

The American author Jon Stephen Fink has written a book dedicated to chicken scenes in movies; there are hundreds and hundreds. How many can you think of?

Connect your project to famous lines and dialogue from movies; numerous examples are imprinted in our memories.

Going to the movies is an excellent form of creative distraction. Adman Francis Glibbery commented: 'When you're stuck on an idea, going to see a film engages your mind with something else creative. Subliminally this can help you see your problem in another context.'

Brainjack
Ideas from movies instantly rerun the emotions engendered in the viewer's mind by the original film. This interacts with the new idea the film has inspired.

Museums

Museums are amazing storehouses of inspiration from all over the world. Enjoy their crazy jumbles and juxtapositions of wonderful objects. They are perfect places in which to immerse yourself in the lineage and descent of ideas while exploring materials, craftsmanship, materials and colour from history and around the globe.

Many decades ago museums were early pioneers of interactivity. Their exhibits offered visitors the opportunity to press buttons, turn handles and switch on lights, triggering a deeper understanding of how the world works.

The Victoria & Albert Museum in London is one of the greatest museums in Europe; it was founded with the mission to collect and display amazing objects in order to inspire British designers and educate the public. Writing on the work of the 1960s psychedelic graphic designers, Michael McNay identified the V&A as a key inspiration 'which nudged the zeitgeist with exhibitions of Aubrey Beardsley and the Czech genius of art nouveau, Alfons Mucha'. See Zeitgeist.

You should be in a museum

Numerous exhibitions have similarly sparked inspiration and caused creativity to head off on new tangents. For example, displays of African tribal art hugely influenced Picasso in the early 1900s and the Paris International Exhibition in 1925 was a catalyst for the Art Deco movement when designers were exposed to exotic creativity from Japan, South America, China and Egypt.

Museum pieces

Photographer William Klein was inspired to use the wax museum in Paris for a series of brilliant fashion photographs; he posed his models as waxworks among real objects. Artist Peter Blake creates mini museums made from collages of found objects and ephemera, some for himself and for his friends (*see* below). His *Museum of the Colour White* is an assembly of objects that range in colour from the purest white to hues approaching black.

An exhibition of 21st-century trash (opposite)
A month's dropped rubbish collected from the forecourt of their design group, displayed by Pali Palavathanan and Michael Johnson.

Peter Blake, *A Museum For Myself*, 1982 (left)
Blake creates a mini museum of his personal treasures. The artwork has evolved over the years as he adds more exhibits. See You! (put yourself in it).

DIY
Visit museums. Go to all their blockbuster temporary exhibitions and get to know their permanent collections. Seek out-of-the-way, strange and wonderful museums and investigate their hidden corners and forgotten exhibits. Visit your local museum – every town has one.

Discover hidden objects – every museum can display only a fraction of its collections; rediscover these hidden gems of inspiration.

Get lost in a museum; you never know what great sources of inspiration you may stumble across.

Our homes are museums of our lives and memories – take inspiration from your unique museum. See You! (put yourself in it).

Brainjack
Collections captivate, and ideas inspired by museums – fusing the past with the present – can cause a viewer's imagination to exhibit an exciting reaction.

Music

Musical and visual creativity are closely linked and music is hugely inspirational to designers and artists. Great visual ideas are said to resonate, chime, strike a chord and hit the right note with viewers – all musical terms. Musicians are described as artists and, like paintings, musical pieces are described as compositions.

Music is a pattern of sounds that is satisfying to a listener. It can be emotionally intense and mood changing. Different arrangements and sequences of notes can connect to the listener so powerfully that they cause physical changes like goose pimples or the hairs on the back of the neck rising. Some musical pieces are instantly uplifting and elating, or at once sad and melancholic, no matter how often we've heard them.

Jamie Dobson, *Record Trace #3*, 2005
Inspired by music, designer and photographer Jamie Dobson created a 'record trace' machine that interprets an entire album or single as a wave form written in light. *See* www.jamiedobson.com

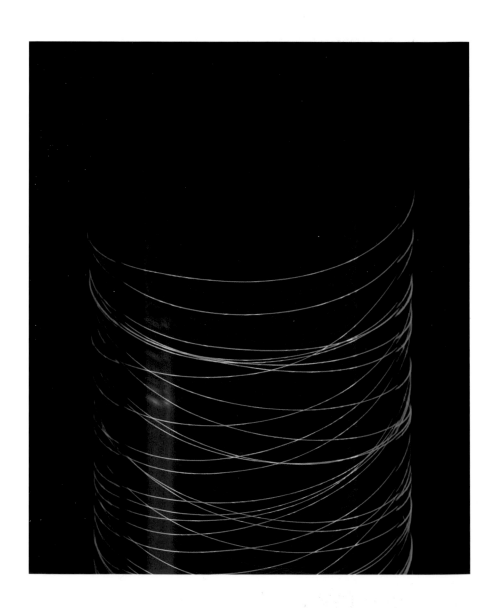

Music and environment
Music reflects the environment in which it was created. You can recognize the hard, concrete sounds of the inner city, the softer sounds of the suburbs and the gentle sounds of music created in rural places.

Graphic inspiration
The notation used to write music has inspired many designers and artists. Crotchets and quavers offer lively and harmonious graphic shapes while the base and treble clef intertwine like instruments.

M

Music

Pop music: powerful condensed emotion

Be inspired by pop music. The most powerful human feelings of joy, love, lust, happiness, unhappiness, loneliness and rejection are the key themes of its hits. It is remarkable that songwriters and musicians are able to condense the most important things in our lives into two- or three-minute recordings.

Pop music has the ability to instantly trigger memories, taking us back to past moments in our lives. Listening to it can at once connect us to an advertisement or film.

Music and painting

Wassily Kandinsky created free abstract paintings that were inspired by classical music: he chose a different colour to signify each emotion it conjured up. He even invented a music machine that translated musical sounds into instructions for composing paintings.

Artist Jackson Pollock's action paintings paralleled his deep love of improvised jazz music. He flicked, poured, spattered and rhythmically dipped paint on to the canvases on the floor of his studio in the way his jazz heroes played their instruments – carefully balancing control, freedom and accidents.

Iconic albums

From the 1950s to the 1980s the dominant design object for most young people was the 12-inch album sleeve. It was often the only place where they could see alternative visual imagery. Its visual impact was critically important to the launch of every new album and designers became famous through their work for different record labels and bands.

The 12-inch LP sleeves are iconic of the decades in which they were designed, from the Blue Note Records jazz sleeves of the 1950s, to Peter Blake's and Jan Haworth's *Sergeant Pepper* cover in the 1960s, Jamie Reid's design for *Never Mind the Bollocks* in the 1970s and Peter Saville's Factory Records sleeves in the 1980s. Handling and studying an album sleeve was a ritual for every music fan.

The move by record companies to showcase music on much smaller-scale cassette tapes and CDs, and now through downloads, has seen the demise of the importance of the iconic single image once seen on album sleeves. Pop videos or promos are now the key way for bands to communicate their identity. *See* Icons.

Cornelius Cardew compositions (left)
English experimental composer Cornelius Cardew created these brilliantly visually expressive radical musical compositions.

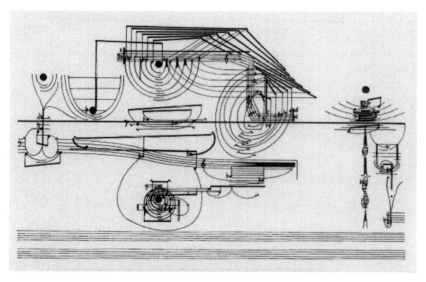

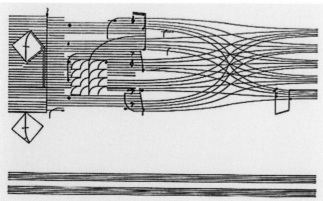

DIY
Explore pop music as a source of inspiration. Link your visual work with music; hitting on a popular song connected to an idea can lead your work to develop in new directions.

Study the work of people inspired by music.

Brainjack
Popular songs are described as being catchy and the choruses are referred to as 'the hook', reflecting how they catch the imagination and draw listeners in. It is thought the patterns of notes used to create music engage large areas of the brain as it attempts to anticipate how sequences and patterns will evolve.

N

Nature

The forms and architecture of the natural world have always inspired and shaped our imagination. Nature's power to create beautiful shapes, rhythms, patterns, structures and colours is extraordinary. Its destructive, malevolent and violent face can be equally compelling.

Matt Walford, Digital Nature (right)
Photographer Matt Walford takes his inspiration from nature, he writes: 'I like taking things apart and putting them back together again: exploring, deconstructing nature, then reconstructing it.' See www.mattwalford.co.uk

Front Design, *Blown vase*, 2009 (below)
Stockholm-based designers Front created this wonderful porcelain vase that appears to be being blown into oblivion by a hurricane, its decoration stretched and smeared, its shape bent and twisted by the power of nature.

'Nature is a great artist, the greatest.'
Brett Weston, photographer

Like artists, sculptors and musicians, numerous designers have transformed the inspiration they have found in nature into ideas in their work. Fashion designer Mark Fast was inspired by the extremes of the natural world, including tempests and thunderstorms, and created a collection based on the intensity of a flash of lightning; the Apple computer mouse is based on a drop of water; Charles Eames and Tom Dixon both based chair designs on the shape of leaves. Other chairs have been based on the forms of pebbles and sea anemones.

DIY
Be a student of nature. Be inspired by its power, forms, intricacy, colours, light, vitality, markings, growth, structures and grids – as a source of both imagery and ideas for construction.

Snowflakes, fossils, skeletons and undersea creatures are great examples of inspirational natural forms.

Brainjack
The power of nature is compelling. Awareness of its omnipresence is deeply impressed into human consciousness.

O

One thing looks like another

Instrumental thinking 1 (below)
A harp appears as thrilling as a rollercoaster in this great ad promoting Classic FM, the UK classical music radio station. The poster was created in 1997 by agency BST, BDDP. Photography by Nadav Kander. *See* www.nadavkander.com.

Instrumental thinking 2, Man Ray, *Violin d'Ingres* (opposite)
Artist and photographer May Ray spotted that the curvaceous shape of his model Kiki echoed the curves of a violin – by painting the f-shaped sound holes onto the print he completed the transformation.

There is a long history of creative people spotting striking visual similarities between objects. In France, in 1832, Charles Philipon was jailed for drawing a satirical caricature of the king as a fat pear – poire is French slang for a dullard. In the court case that followed he was acquitted after he asked the jury, 'Is it my fault if His Majesty looks like a pear?' and drew a series of sketches that demonstrated the resemblance was undeniable.

Picasso exhibited bicycle saddles that look like bull's and monkey's heads: he simply displayed the saddles upright to show the visual coincidence. Salvador Dalí playfully sculpted his moustache into a dollar sign for publicity photographs, a witty visual riposte to critics who had christened him Avida Dollars – an anagram of his name indicating he was 'avid for money'. Dalí also enlarged actress Mae West's puffed lips into a design for a curvaceous sofa, and transformed objects and landscapes into figures and faces in many of his paintings. See Caricature, Making faces, Satire.

EXHILARATION

Boddingtons beer ad (this page)
The foamy head of Boddingtons beer is transformed into a rocker's quiff in this smart 1994 ad created by agency Bartle Bogle Hegarty.

JI footballs (opposite top left)
A drain cover becomes a soccer ball in this poster for a street football festival.

Broccoli dumb-bell (opposite top right)
Broccoli becomes a dumb-bell for this ad on the benefits of eating your greens. It was shot by photographer Cleon Daniel. *See* www.cleondaniel.com

Burger belly (opposite middle right)
Photographer Lauren Mitton created this burger belly for a campaign on the downsides of consuming too much fast food. *See* www.laurenmitton.co.uk

Preparation H (opposite bottom left)
The agony of piles is vividly visualized as one thing looks like another in this very discomforting 2010 ad for haemorrhoid cream.

Source mouth (opposite bottom right)
In this spicy Brazillian ad for Parmalot Hot Sauce the ketchup bottle makes a perfect fiery mouth. It was created by agency DM9 DDB Publicidade in 1999.

One thing looks like another

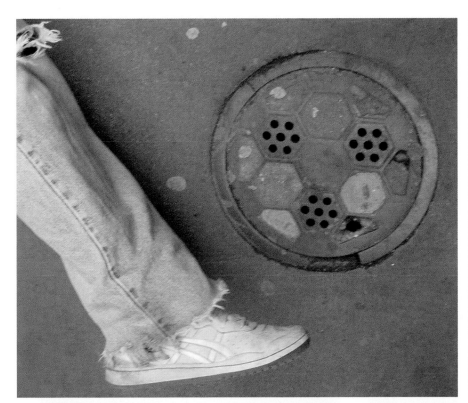

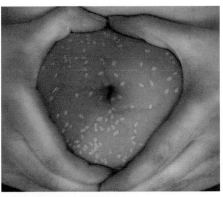

BE PREPARED | PREPARATION **H** HEMORRHOIDAL *OINTMENT*

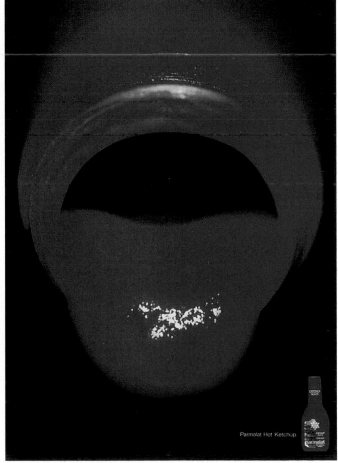

Parmalat Hot Ketchup

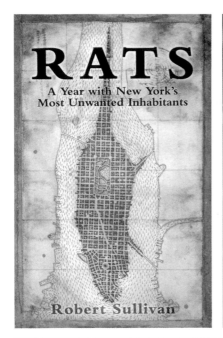

LONDON. MADE FOR CYCLING.
You're better off by bike. Visit tfl.gov.uk/cycling

MAYOR OF LONDON

Y⊖UR
Transport for London

Grow your own ad, 1942 (opposite)
Designer Abram Games brilliantly made
use of the visual similarities he had spotted
between the look of a spade and that of the
front of a ship in this poster encouraging
citizens to grow their own food rather than
buy imported goods. The shapes of the
spade and the ship, the soil and the sea,
the handle and the smoke from the funnel
perfectly integrate and juxtapose in this
totally hand-drawn poster created for the
British War Office in 1942. *See* Garage
Genius, Juxtaposition.

***Rats*, book cover (top left)**
The aerial view of Manhattan is redrawn to
reveal the city's most unloved resident on
the cover of Robert Sullivan's 2004 book.

Game control (top right)
Nipples become computer game control
buttons in this 1999 ad created by Trevor
Beattie – perfectly combining the twin
obsessions of adolescents.

Cycling London (above)
Recycling the London skyline.

 DIY
Discover the visual possibilities
of your subject matter. Connect
the subject visually to what you
wish to communicate.

 Brainjack
Viewers are engaged by the
transformation of one object
into another. The similarities
or differences between them
communicate the idea as the
viewer's imagination flickers
between the two.

P

Photographs

We have seen certain photographs so often that they are imprinted on our minds. This stored common knowledge means their compositions can be reused for instant communication.

The windswept head-shot of beret-wearing revolutionary Che Guevara conveys idealism and heroism, and has been re-created many times in attempts to transfer these qualities to other individuals. When a famous photograph is reused in an unexpected context, some of the power of the original is hard-wired into any recreation. See Icons.

The Girls, *Self Portrait as Princes William and Harry* (above)
Artists Zoe Sinclair and Andrea Blood, known as the Girls, often explore Englishness in their work – here creating a self portrait inspired by a saccharine official royal photo. *See* www.thegirls.co.uk

The Spectator, Keeler cover (right)
Ad for the British magazine *The Spectator* recreating Lewis Morley's infamous 1963 photo of Christine Keeler. Use of Morley's photograph instantly conveys sex, politics and scandal – *The Observer Book of Scandal* noted that the 'photograph has become a short-hand image for everything that is wickedly good, and wonderfully bad.'

 DIY
Use the power of well-known photographs. Distil the message you wish to communicate and take inspiration from famous existing images that express what you wish to say.

 Brainjack
When a famous photograph is reused in an unexpected way the viewer does a visual double take. Some of the power imprinted into the original is hard-wired into any re-creation.

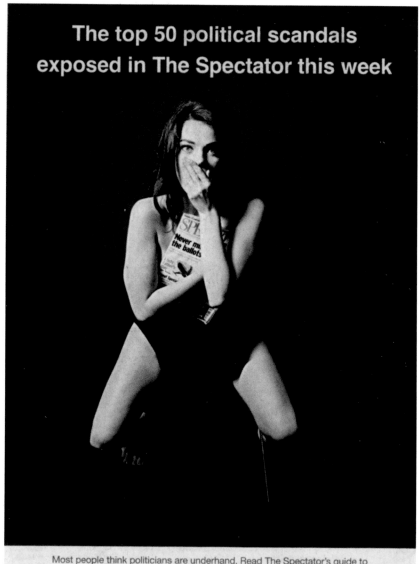

The top 50 political scandals exposed in The Spectator this week

Most people think politicians are underhand. Read The Spectator's guide to the top 50 political scandals and you'll realise they're cheats, liars and adulterers, too.

THE SPECTATOR
Champagne for the brain
On Sale Now

Photography

Photography is inspiring as it can give tangible and permanent impressions of a world we can never see with our own eyes. We see our surroundings in real time, in real colour and mostly at eye level. The wonder of photography is that it can reveal and record time in many different slices, see the world from many different viewpoints, and record what is seen at different magnifications and in a multitude of different colours.

Thea Swayne, Electromagnetic portraits, 2004
Swayne's photographs reveal the invisible emanation that surrounds us all. She focused on creative young people at the Royal College of Art in London using a camera invented in the early 1980s by American Guy Coggins. A multidisciplinary designer, Swayne wonderfully describes herself as an 'ideamonger'. *See* www. theaswayne.co.uk

Seeing in new ways

Photography can help us to see the tiniest objects at a huge scale and the most distant ones in close-up. It can change colours, show things in greater contrast or in black and white. The camera is a brilliant creative tool that can be used to direct the viewer's eye by selectively focusing on specific objects, or showing the subject of a photograph out of focus or in incredible detail.

Cameras can record levels and types of light that are beyond the scope of the human eye. Examples are infrared and ultraviolet radiation, heat and x-rays. *See* X-rays.

Photography triggers ideas

The images photography has given to the world can be hugely inspirational. An example is Eadweard Muybridge's series of photographs of people and animals in motion, which have inspired generations of designers and artists;
they are still in print today over 130 years after their creation. Through Muybridges's sequences it was possible to see the exact flow and rhythm of human and animal movement for the first time. He was an amazing technical innovator: to create his most famous images, of a horse in motion, he used banks of cameras whose shutters were attached to taut threads that were broken as the galloping horse passed them, causing the shutters to snap in sequence. Muybridge's photos have been utilized by Edgar Degas, Picasso, Jasper Johns, Francis Bacon, Andy Warhol and numerous other artists.

All ideas are doable

Even the most complex ideas can be executed in a totally convincing manner using digital photography and retouching. No idea is undoable.

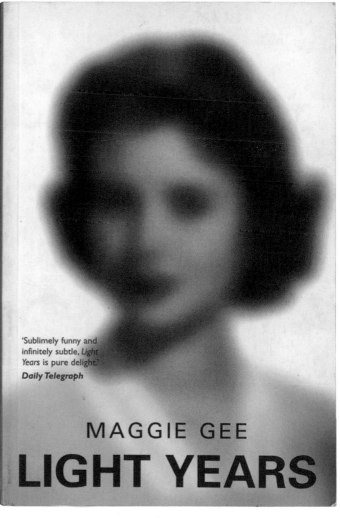

Polo ad (opposite)
While our eyes sharply focus on everything we look at, the camera can selectively focus on things at the exclusion of all others – this is used to great effect in this 1998 ad for Volkswagen created by agency BMP DDB.

Light car (above)
Photography can record things we could otherwise never see – this image of a car was created by art students Jacob Russell and Lizzie Ayre.

Maggie Gee book cover (right)
The camera can see the world unfocused – used here to create a striking book cover.

'Sublimely funny and infinitely subtle, *Light Years* is pure delight.'
Daily Telegraph

MAGGIE GEE
LIGHT YEARS

Minnie Weisz, *room 303 camera obscura* **(above),** *norfolk suite camera obscura* **(opposite)**

Over 500 years ago people had discovered that a small hole in the wall of a darkened room could act as a lens causing images of the scene outside to appear inverted on the opposite wall. The phenomenon was named 'camera obscura'– meaning dark room – this is how the camera got its name. Inspired by the effect, artist Minnie Weisz created these haunting images of the Kings Cross area of London, sealing the windows of condemned houses except for tiny pinholes that let the buildings outside project onto the shabby walls and abandoned possessions of former occupants. She recorded the scenes – invisible to the human eye at this intensity – using a conventional camera and long exposures. See www. minnieweisz.co.uk

Ten inspirational photographers
Every creative person should
know the work of:

Erwin Blumenfeld
Henri Cartier-Bresson
Elliott Erwitt
William Klein
Nick Knight
Jacques-Henri Lartigue
Angus McBean
Sarah Moon
Irving Penn
Hiroshi Sugimoto.

'Photographs are not only
points of reference, they're
often triggers for ideas.'
Francis Bacon, artist

'Photography is a magical thing.'
Jacques-Henri Lartigue, photographer

 DIY
Be inspired by photography that
records the world in new and
different ways. Be inspired by the
work of famous photographers.

Take your own photographs and
always carry a camera. Creative
photography involves selecting
the right camera and lens to
express your ideas, coupled with
careful consideration of viewpoint,
composition, crop, focus, depth
of field, exposure time, lighting,
image quality, colour, contrast
and post-production using
a computer.

Experiment with both conventional
and unconventional photographic
cameras and imagery. As well as
using all formats of digital and
film-based cameras try working
with instant-imaging cameras,
photocopiers and scanners.

Brainjack
Photographs that reveal the
world in new ways can remain
in the memory for ever.

  Further viewing
See also images by Etienne–
Jules Marey whose studies of
movement inspired Marcel
Duchamp's famous painting
Nude Descending a Staircase.

Photo-
typography

Photographers and designers have always loved the chance discovery of accidentally formed letters in the street or natural world. Many have taken this as inspiration to create phototypography. All kinds of different objects have been used to make the shapes of letters, including arrangements of people, food, flowers and toys.

Horst *Vogue* cover, 1940 (right)
Horst P. Horst creates brilliant fashion phototypography with Swedish supermodel Lisa Fonssagrives for this memorable magazine cover.

Flowers alphabet (opposite top)
Matt Walford's floral phototypography.
See Nature, www.mattwalford.co.uk

Tools alphabet (opposite bottom left)
Mervyn Kurlansky's 1977 alphabet of tools and objects used by designers.

Bulldog (opposite bottom right)
Dave Wood's fabulous bulldog clip alphabet. The discovery that an object creates a letterform can lead to the great adventure of trying to complete an entire A–Z.

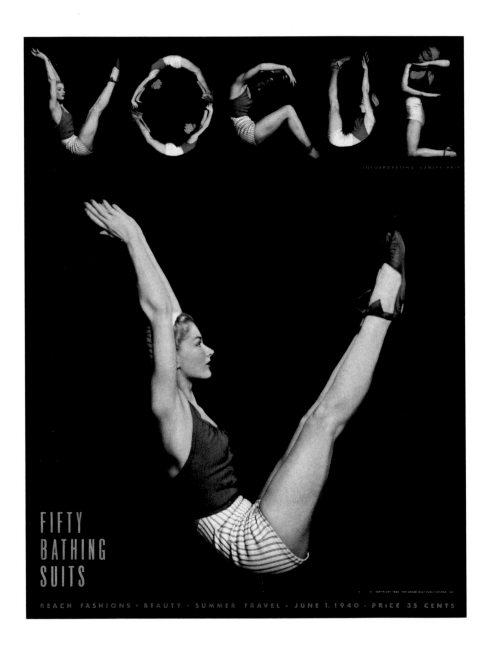

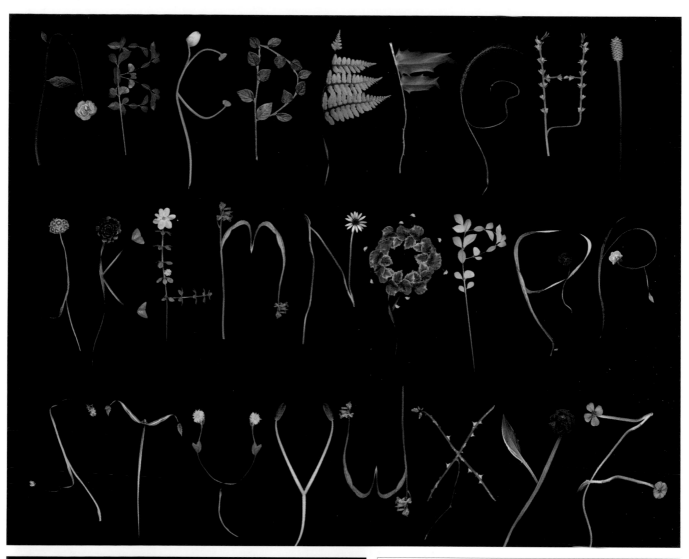

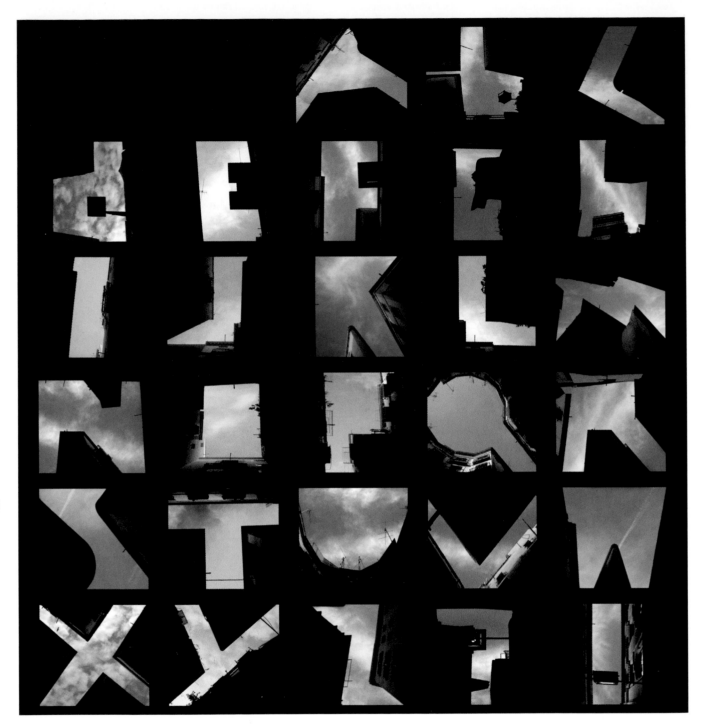

Sky alphabet (above)
Lisa Rienermann's wonderful sky alphabet.
'Standing in a little courtyard in Barcelona
I looked up. I saw houses, the sky, clouds
and a Q. The negative space in-between
the houses formed a letter. I loved the idea
of the sky as words, the negative being the
positive. If I could find a Q other letters
should be somewhere around the corner.
In the following weeks, I kept running around
looking up to the sky. Bit by bit I found all
the letters of the alphabet.'
See www.lisarienermann.com

Letterforms (top left)
A page of found letterforms in a student sketchbook. *See* Sketchbooks and notebooks.

Martin Parr, *Objects* **book cover (top right)**
Some of photographer Martin Parr's collections of kitsch create the title of his 2008 book. *See* So bad it's great.

Hello (ccntre)
Matt Walford says Hello in this phototopiary. *See* www.mattwalford.co.uk

Joss McKinley (right centre)
Photographer Joss McKinley created this poignant installation in the window of a gallery exhibiting his work using fresh chrysanthemums. During the four weeks of the show the petals slowly wilted and fell. *See* www.jossmckinley.com

Bis typography (above left)
The logo of Bis publishing is graphically recreated using their books.

China poster (above right)
Layabout photography students created this poster for an exhibition of pictures taken on a study trip to East Asia. Photo by Matt Frederick and Dave Stokes. *See* www.mattfrederick.co.uk, www. davestokesphotography.com

 DIY
Transform your subject by spelling it out. Collect accidentally formed letters as sources of inspiration.

 Brainjack
An exciting tension is created between the words that are spelled out and what is used to create them. The two elements are satisfyingly fused in the viewer's imagination.

Alexander Shields, *God, Job, Work, Rave,* 2005-06
These installations were created in abandoned London buildings using materials discovered at each site. *God, Job* and *Rave* were photographed by William Eckersley in 2006. *Work* was created with Jimmy Turrell in 2005. See www.leftlondon.co.uk

Places of worship

Places of worship are a key source of inspiration for many creative people. The images created by artists Gilbert and George have the bright, vivid colours and thick black demarcation of the hand-blown glass and leading in stained-glass windows in churches and cathedrals. Jeff Koons is inspired by the drama, passion and symbolism of the religious art and sculpture in Catholic places of worship in Italy. Pierre et Gilles find inspiration in the compositions, colours and sensuality of Hinduism, Buddhism and Sikhism in India.

The symmetry, infinitely repeating patterns and geometric designs of Islamic art in the tiles, brickwork and carpets of mosques inspired Escher (see Maths) and designer William Morris, who wrote 'Persia has become a Holy Land' to pattern designers.

Pierre et Gilles, *Sarasvati*, **1988 (right)**
Pierre Commoy and Gilles Blanchard, better known as Pierre et Gilles, have created many sumptuous hand-coloured photographs inspired by the religions of the world. Here they take influence from South Asian places of worship, having become enthralled by Hindu, Buddhist and Sikh religious art during trips to India.

DIY
When travelling, seek out places of worship as well as galleries and museums, and discover ideas and inspiration within them. The paraphernalia of worship can also be inspiring.

Brainjack
The art and design in places of worship are powerful as they echo the intense devotion of believers.

Puns

A pun is the playful, often humorous, exploitation of two different meanings of the same word or of words or phrases that sound similar.

In England shopkeepers delight in using puns to name their establishments. There are hairdressers called Curl Up and Dye and Hair Apparent; fish and chip takeaways named The Rock & Sole Plaice, There's a Plaice for Us and I Love What You've Done with the Plaice; clothes shops called Gone to Blaiser's and Bitchin' Slacks!; pet shops named Paws for Thought; and a bathroom supplier called That Sinking Feeling.

Sub-editors on newspapers frequently create punning headlines that utilize commonly known song and book titles: articles on the Ealing area of west London have been titled Sexual Ealing and Give My Regards to Ealing Broadway, a feature on a rock band on the road was headed Cider with Roadies, and a retro fashion story was titled The Way We Wore. Visual developments of verbal puns can be equally playful.

Love Handles (above)
This display wittily exploits visual and verbal meanings and coincidences between illy's espresso cups and the bikini-clad model.

At last solved… (below)
A Christmas card punningly reveals that Santa shot JFK.

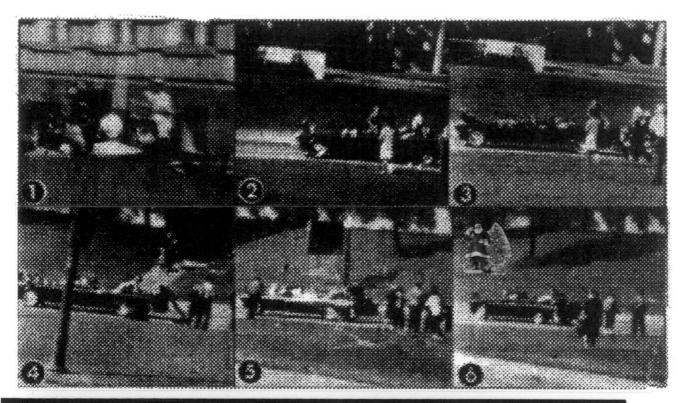

AT LAST SOLVED................THE MAN ON THE GRASSY NOEL

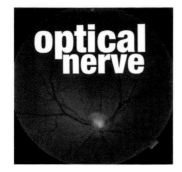

optical nerve

John Brewer, Optical Nerve, exhibition poster, 2011 (above)

A visionary pun created by art director and teaching guru John Brewer for an exhibition of experimental student photographs. The two different meanings of the title – the fibres that transmit information from the eye to the brain and visual bravado – are united in the photograph, a remarkable image of the inside of the human eye. *See* Eyes, Science.

Needled (right)

The orgiastic nature of modern Christmas celebrations is sent up by this pun. The design was inspired by Richard Hamilton's famous 1956 pop art collage *Just What Is It that Makes Today's Homes So Different, So Appealing? See* Art.

'Love means never having to say you're from Surrey.'

Michael Palin, comic

DIY

Collect puns. Find them within the language of your work and develop them verbally and visually; words are pregnant with double, triple or multiple meanings. Use dictionaries and a thesaurus to find alternative definitions and spellings; discover hidden similarities between words and new connections and cross connections between words and phrases. *See* Wordplay.

Brainjack

Puns communicate the realization that the world can be seen in more than one way. They appeal to the viewer's knowledge and humour – and can be really clever. The reverberation created by a double meaning can rebound in the mind for a long time.

DON'T YOU JUST HATE VACUUMING UP

THE NEEDLES AFTER CHRISTMAS

P

Puns

Q
Questions

Art aims to ask questions of viewers, in particular about big subjects such as 'What is our purpose?' and 'What happens when we die?' Questions can make people think. Creating one opens a conversation with the viewer, as it asks for a reply. A dialogue is presumed, which makes communication seem more personal.

Robert Stadler, ?, 2007
Austrian artist Robert Stadler asks questions of worshippers in this installation first created in Paris in 2007. He wrote: 'Visitors enter the church through a lateral door and first see a scattered group of luminous spheres hovering in the choir. As one approaches the centre of the nave, the spheres form a giant question mark. They become a punctuation mark superimposed over the religious symbols. Then as one moves through the church, the question mark decomposes. The figure becomes abstracted again in order to echo the hanging lights of the cathedral. Contrasting with the symmetry of the edifice, these luminous suspension points are like a musical notation, or holes punctuating the architectural volume. The question (or doubt) is absorbed by the space.' This artwork has since been exhibited in places of worship around the world. *See* www.robertstadler.net

DIY
Communicate by asking questions.

Brainjack
Our inbuilt desire to understand things and make sense of the world is sparked by questions. Viewers become engaged by the question and then by striving for an answer.

A winning question
An award-winning advertising campaign for Volkswagen asked: 'Have you ever wondered how the man that drives the snowplow… drives to the snowplow?'

R

Reinvention

To reinvent is to radically change and create entirely anew. Often a customary way of doing things remains unchallenged – leading to things like magazines, shop windows and exhibitions looking pretty much the same. Reinvention should be constant as there are no rules or boundaries – only conventions, as photographer Bill Brandt remarked about his creative discipline – 'it is not a sport, it doesn't have a book of rules'. You cannot be offside or sent off for foul play in creativity.

Spray dress (right)
Alexander McQueen brilliantly reinvented the fashion show in 1999 when two industrial paint spraying robots danced balletically with a model spinning on a turntable before beautifully decorating her dress. See this amazing event on youtube.

Heatherwick windows (below)
Thomas Heatherwick's 1997 reinvention of department store windows.
See Digitality, www.heatherwick.com

Reinventing the exhibition

The Dutch design group Droog reinvented the exhibition when they created the Droog Hotel. At a design festival in Milan, rather than booking a conventional gallery in which to display their work they temporarily took over a down-on-its-luck hotel for the week of the show. On entering, visitors were met by Droog staff dressed in hotel uniforms; they were asked to register as guests and were then ushered to different floors to view the group's latest furniture and product designs installed in rooms and suites.

Viewing the witty, innovative designs in shabby surroundings, coupled with the theatricality of the human interaction between vistiors and the Droog staff – who maintained the pretence that they were obsequious hotel employees – created a memorable effect, and news of this great exhibition spread rapidly round the festival. *See* Word of mouth.

Reinventing the wheel

Designer Mike Burrows reinvented the bicycle. Throughout its history its frames featured front and back forks that hold the wheels in place; Burrows' design featured a single arm at front and rear. This reduced the weight of the bicycle. It could be speedily folded for carrying and storage, and the wheels could be changed with far greater ease than previously. *See* Counter-intuition.

Reinventing magazines

Most magazines are formulaic: the visual conventions are that they arc around A4 (8.3 × 11.7 inches) in size, and are bound down the left edge, with a life-size smiling face on the cover beneath the logo. Content begins with the editor's introduction which is followed by a mix of news, features and interviews. These are interspersed with advertising which helps to pay the bills. Each issue pretty much mirrors the previous one in design, stance and opinion. *Visionaire* smashed this mould. Every issue of the magazine was morphed in size, shape, format and content; the only constant factor was its name. There was even an issue that featured only smells. *See* Sensations.

Reinventing shop window displays

Where the windows of most stores are changed seasonally, the ones in fashion designer Paul Smith's shops provide ever-changing displays of must-see ideas. Cognoscenti divert their journeys in order to see them. Always surprising, they feature joyful juxtapositions and unexpected interactions between his latest products. Smith says: 'Sometimes they change daily. And that means all my shop windows, from New York to Hong Kong. You've got to catch people's attention. The windows are as important as my catwalk shows in London and Paris.'

Thomas Heatherwick created traffic-stopping windows for Harvey Nichols department store in London when he designed a massive, multisurfaced laminated wood structure that twisted and flowed both inside and outside the windows (*see* opposite below).

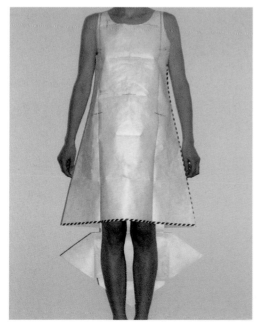
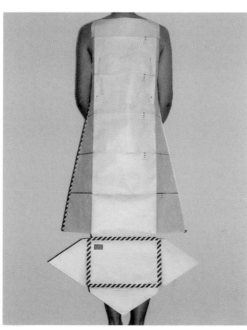

Postal dress (left)
Multidisciplinary designers Rebecca Brown and Mike Heath push the creative envelope. *See* www.rebccooandmike.com

DIY
Examine conventions, then smash them.

Brainjack
Radically changing the appearance, form or presentation of something seizes the viewer's imagination. Recognizing reinvention is exciting as concepts that are taken to be fundamental have been altered, maybe forever.

Rescaling

In two of the world's most imaginative books the familiar world is subverted by the unexpected sizing of everyday objects – both hugely enlarged and greatly reduced. In Gulliver's Travels, *Lilliput is a world where everything is one-twelfth the size of our own, whilst in Brobdingnag everything is twelve times bigger. Similarly in* Alice's Adventures in Wonderland *Alice finds herself in a world of huge then tiny objects. A massive change of scale can grip the imagination.*

Downscaling (above)
The size of this tiny portfolio made it stand out from a crowd of normal-sized ones at a student graduation show.

Upscaling 1 (right)
Swedish-born artist Claes Oldenburg creates stunning sculptures by enormously enlarging mundane objects and fast food. He has super-sized burgers and fries, ice creams, sandwiches and cakes. He refers to the resizing in the titles, calling the objects scale A, B, C, etc, as if they could be ordered from a take-away menu or catalogue. This is his 12.5-metre high *Trowel Scale B*, made in 1971, one of a series of enormous workman's tools.

Upscaling 2 (opposite)
American artist Jeff Koons' amazing 13-metre high topiary West Highland terrier puppy stands guard outside the Guggenheim Museum in Bilbao. It was created in 1992. *See* So bad it's good.

Blow-ups

Artists including Claes Oldenburg, Roy Lichtenstein, Jeff Koons and Damien Hirst have rescaled everyday objects and images, and created massive hamburgers, hot dogs, cartoons, dogs and children's toys.

Seeing the shrink

Photographers Helmut Newton and David LaChappelle used tiny cars and coffee cups in their advertisements for Volkswagen and Lavazza coffee. Well, that's what it looks like, though they may have used normally sized cars and cups and gigantic human models.

New Orleans Warhol (above)
Revellers at New Orleans Mardi Gras created these unforgettable outfits further scaling up the enlargement of Campbell's soup cans made by Andy Warhol. *See* Art.

Stop the guns (left)
In this billboard campaign targeting UK gun crime the massive rescaling of the weapon in proportion to the mobile phone triggers an unsettling tension between the two. The graphic simplicity of the image communicates the message with great clarity.

 DIY
Experiment with the scale of the objects in your brief. Accentuate the scale of the ones that are most vital to your message.

 Brainjack
The imagination is stimulated when the expected order of the world is changed and new possibilities are suggested. Enlargement can inspire awe or expand on an idea.

 Further viewing
In the Laurel and Hardy film *Brats*, the duo play two fathers and their naughty kids. When they play the children, chairs and toys are massive; when they play the adults, everything is normal size.

Reversing problems

A great idea is sometimes described as having turned a problem on its head. Looking at the reverse of a problem can reveal new ways of thinking that may lead to an answer or fresh ideas.

Food exhibition (above)
Attempting to reverse the problem of always having a huge mess to tidy up after art student exhibitions, tutors set this project in which food was the only creative material allowed, hoping that the entire show could be eaten leaving nothing to clean up. *See* Materials.

Reverse thinking

Pickpocketing is a problem. *Reverse*: Put messages in people's pockets by stealth to warn them of this problem.

Tattoos deteriorate with age as the colour fades and the drawing blurs. *Reverse*: Create tattoos that improve with age as the colour fades and the drawing blurs.

'I'm sick of clearing up at the end of every student art exhibition.' *Reverse*: Create an exhibition made of food which is eaten during the show – result, exciting exhibition and no clearing up. *See* Sensations.

'I am arranging a summer outside event (concert/picnic/wedding, etc.) and there is a chance rain may spoil the day.' *Reverse*: Design the event so that rainfall makes the day.

'I can't speak French.' *Reverse*: 'I know hundreds of French words already – *café, bar, chic, cinema, cuisine, enfant terrible, fait accompli, tour de force, bête noire,* etc. – I just need to know how to join them up.'

'I have no budget.' *Reverse*: 'The things I already have are perfect for the job.' *See* Garage genius.

'The structure is ugly and has to be hidden by decoration.' *Reverse*: Make the structure beautiful and dispense with the expense of decoration. This 'reverse' is exemplified in the million-selling Anglepoise lamp – now regarded as a masterpiece of design.

Museums prevent people touching objects by displaying them behind glass and employing battalions of security guards. *Reverse*: Show objects that visitors can be encouraged to touch.

'The downside of the seaside resort I have to promote is that it's much chillier than its competitors.' *Reverse*: 'Skegness is so bracing'; the poster for a town on Britain's North Sea coast.

'The car I have to advertise is really quite small.' *Reverse*: 'It makes your house look bigger'; copy line that turns the problem on its head to create a smart and witty Volkswagen advertisement.

'Art is about creation and its venue is a gallery.' *Reverse*: Make art about destruction and do it in a shop. British-born artist Michael Landy destroyed everything he owned – all 7,229 possessions – in an industrial crusher in an old C&A department store in Oxford Street in London.

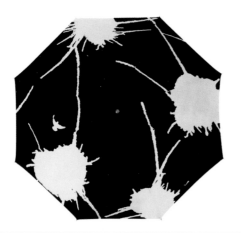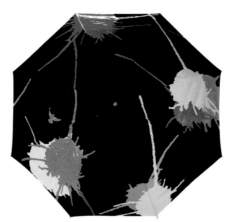

Squidarella (left)
Emma-Jayne Parkes and Viviane Jaeger, partners in the creative company Squid London, designed this great umbrella reversing the idea that rain spoils the day. It uses a material that changes from monochrome to vivid colour when wet. They call it the Squidarella. They write: 'We are a creative think-tank. Our cauldron of ideas is simmering!'
See www.squidlondon.com

Travelling show (above)
Wishing to take an impressive exhibition of their work on an exchange trip to a Photography College in East Asia, students found the expense of printing, framing and transportation, together with the difficulty of hanging and lighting a show in an unfamiliar environment were barriers to success. Reversing these thoughts – let's not print, not frame, not pay to transport, and hang the hanging and lighting – led the students to created a 'travelling show' of specially shot stereoscopic images displayed in these stereoviewers.

S

Satire

Satire is the attack dog of comedy, the pit bull that can sink its teeth into the the high and mighty, and draw blood. It is a weapon the powerless can use against the powerful; it takes the side of the little guy against the bully. One satirist described his job as 'comforting the afflicted and afflicting the comfortable'.

'*Satire is dark, uncomfortable, challenging and threatening.*'

Rory Bremner, comedian

Gerald Scarfe, *Ken Relieves Congestion*, 2003
In this drawing Gerald Scarfe ridicules the former mayor of London Ken Livingstone as a drunken clown who talks out of his arse – *see* Expressions Visualized. The punning title twists the knife, implying Livingstone has the shits, and referring to his scheme aimed at unblocking central London by charging cars to enter. *See* Puns, Caricature, Making Maps

 DIY
Unleash the pit bull of satire on the targets you feel cry out for attack. Be vicious. Go for the jugular. Take no prisoners in revealing the failures of society; bring the high and mighty down to earth with a bang using satire as your weapon. Target injustice. Crusade. Give a voice to the little guy and those who struggle. Study the political cartoons in daily newspapers that comment satirically on topical events. Look at the drawings of Steve Bell and the television and movie work of master satirist and comedic anarchist Chris Morris. *See* Caricature.

 Brainjack
Satire features an empowering lack of respect for authority, the status quo and taste. By provoking laughter at something or somebody you rob them of their power. George Orwell wrote that 'every joke is a tiny revolution'; during the instant in which satire communicates an audience feels a momentary mental superiority to their enemy or oppressor. By laughing at our worst fears we make them temporarily ridiculous.

Science

The word science derives from the Latin word for knowledge. Scientists are knowledge builders who increase and extend our understanding of the world through methodical experimentation. Though this rigorous process of testing to provide reliable facts – giving rise to laws, such as those of motion, gravity and nature – seems at odds with the playful, mercurial world of creativity, science can be a wonderful source of creative inspiration.

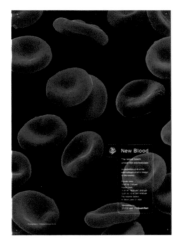

New Blood poster (above)
A scanning electron microscope with the power to magnify by factors up to 250,000 recorded this amazing image of individual human blood cells used for a poster for New Blood – an exhibition showcasing the work of graphic design, visual communication, advertising, digital media, illustration and photography graduates.

Birmingham ballet poster (right)
Thermal imaging cameras were developed by scientists to aid fire fighters in seeing through smoke and darkness. Here one was used to create a great 2007 poster communicating the Birmingham Ballet is hot. *See* Creative Collisions.

Jon Quinnell, *World Stability Table* (opposite)
Inspired by the periodic table in which the elements are ranked and interrelated, art student Jon Quinnell created the *World Stability Table*.

A gift from science
Neon lighting is a gift from science that changed the night-time appearance of the world's cities for ever when designers saw that its bright luminescence made it possible to produce vivid, pulsing and glowing advertising and signage. *See* Digitality, Materials.

BIRMINGHAM
Feel the heat

19 Nutcrackers, 7 Swan Lakes, 5 Giselles and over 54,000 seats for lovers of dance.

www.visitbirmingham.com/arts

It's rocket science

The space race of the 1960s and 1970s provided inspiration for numerous artists, designers, fashion designers, writers, film-makers and musicians. The entire world was inspired in 1972 when astronauts on Apollo 17 beamed photographs back from the moon. What caught the public's imagination were not the pictures of the moon itself – most of which were unexciting – but a single image known as 'the blue marble' which showed the Earth; we could see ourselves for the first time.

Scientific inspiration

British artist Roger Hiorns created an installation, *Seizure*, that brought to mind science experiments at school – but at an extraordinary scale. He made an amazing, vivid blue crystalline cave in a condemned block of flats in London, using industrial quantities of copper sulphate. This was mixed with water, pumped into a sealed flat and allowed to crystallize. Viewers walked through rooms whose walls and ceilings were encrusted with massive, glittering and frosty geometrical shapes created during the crystallization process. *See* Reinvention, Rescaling.

Current thinking

Harry Beck took inspiration for his 1931 design of the London Underground map from electrical diagrams; these express connections with great simplicity and precision, as any mistake can be fatal. In Beck's revolutionary map all the stations appear more or less equidistant and aligned – he dispensed with exact geography and measurements of distances in exchange for clarity. His now iconic map (*see* Icons) has been copied around the world.

Scientific language

The visual language of science has inspired numerous creative people. For example, the periodic table of chemical elements has been used by artists Keith Tyson and Damien Hirst, art student Jon Quinnell (*see* below), and redesigned to advertise Volkswagen cars.

Creativity and the evils of science

Brilliant work has been created in response to, and campaigning against, the dark side of science. This includes flags for the Campaign for Nuclear Disarmament (*see* Flags) and unforgettable advertisements designed to sway public opinion against the use of live animals in scientific and medical experiments.

The mad scientist is a popular character in literature and movies; an early prototype was Dr Frankenstein, created by the writer Mary Shelley.

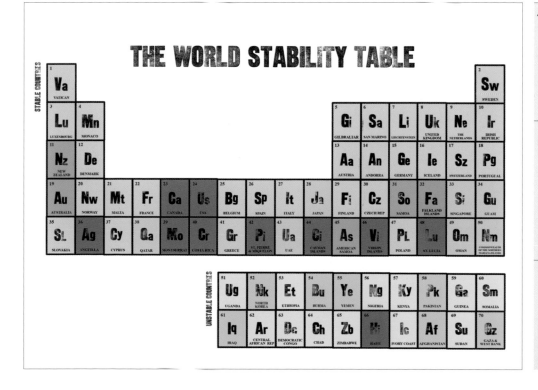

DIY
Be inspired by the forces science has discovered, such as magnetism and gravity, and the new types of image it has gifted to us through the microscope and endoscope. Find inspiration in the latest scientific discoveries and creative uses for the tools of science. See X-rays.

Brainjack
The word 'science' comes from the Latin for knowledge, and scientists reveal new worlds as they strive to know more about all aspects of life. Science expands our minds as it simultaneously looks ever more closely at the tiny particles we are made of, and ever further away at the gigantic universe in which our planet spins.

Further viewing
See brilliant anti-nuclear posters by F.H.K. Henrion and Peter Kennard.

Sensations

The imagination can be stimulated not just by the mind's eye but also by the mind's ear, tastes and feelings. Non-visual sensations are immensely powerful; everyone is nostalgic for the taste of the confectionery of their childhood, can instantly recall the smell of the family car, and who doesn't love popping bubble wrap?

Liu Dao, *Cranky Little Fellas*, 2010 (above and opposite)

Ornate curtained wooden birdcages are a common sight in the streets of China, art collective Liu Dao created this unforgettable installation in a leading Shanghai gallery, hanging a series of them from branches that appeared to sprout from the walls. The cranky little fellas of the title are the stuffed birds that can just be glimpsed inside; the temptation to raise the curtains to see them clearly is irresistible. This causes the birds to unleash a torrent of abuse at visitors – they shout '**** you and your ugly boyfriend' and 'keep walking you dumb sack of ****'. The effect on gallery visitors is remarkable, some are shocked, some burst into laughter while others are offended at hearing obscenities in the normally sober environment of an art gallery.

Sound and action

In an art school project, 'random acts of education', students were challenged to create inexpensive, unthreatening small objects that would be left on public transport and would enlighten the people who found them. Schway Whar placed educational messages, each accompanied by a tiny bell, inside matchboxes, and explained: 'Instinctively on coming across a stray matchbox on the bus or train you will rattle it to see if its empty – if instead of making a rattle-rattle sound it surprisingly goes ding-a-ling-a-ling, you're definitely going to open it and find the message.'

Sound has been used in attempts to calm or stir up crowds, end sieges and increase shoppers' spending. It has also been a creative material for artists.

Sound: pictures in the imagination

Radio can create incredible pictures in the imagination by combining sound and voices. In 1938 Orson Welles' radio production of *The War of the Worlds* did this so successfully that much of the United States was thrown into a panic when listeners believed the world was being invaded by creatures from other planets. Welles apologised but was signed up by Hollywood on the strength of the hoax.

Taste sensations

Crunchy, crisp, sour, bitter, sweet and salty are all adjectives used to describe food. Chefs can be outstandingly creative, combining ingredients, textures and flavours in new and unexpected ways to make taste masterpieces. Art students have put on edible exhibitions using food as their creative material – with the aim of creating a show that required no clearing up when it ended as all the exhibits had been eaten (*see* Reversing problems).

Though the language of cookery has been applied to ideas – Korean artist Bohnchang Koo described putting them 'on the shelf for a while to allow them time to rise, like bread does once the yeast is added' – in the English language the food expression most widely used to describe ideas is 'half baked'.

Smell: an instant trigger

Smell is hugely evocative and can instantly trigger memories. Film-makers have experimented with smell-o-vision in which scratch and sniff cards were given to cinema goers. These were smelt at key points during films to add another sensory dimension to the visual experience. Record companies have tried releasing scratch and sniff album covers, including ones that featured the scent of flowers – and some that smelt of rubber tyres.

Advertisers have targeted cinema goers by pumping the smell of freshly made food through air conditioning to coincide with the action and dialogue in commercials, while nightclubs and the band Throbbing Gristle have experimented with releasing aromas, perfumes and behaviour-influencing pheromones during live performances.

Touch: feel the feeling

Sensations come through any communication with the body. Film-makers have experimented with turning the heat up and down in cinemas during movies to accompany images of great warmth or cold, while changing the texture of the surface on which visitors stand has been used in many exhibitions. The effect of being on an unexpected one such as pebbles, gravel, sand, grass or AstroTurf can greatly change the experience of viewing images.

DIY
Cause a sensation. Make your ideas appeal to the ear, nose and touch of your audience as well as to their eyes.

Brainjack
Harnessing sensations can take people outside themselves and into other worlds. Communication is generally visual and verbal; utilizing other avenues to connect to people can make your message far more exciting. Sensations can pierce an audience's defences.

Shadows

A person or object juxtaposed with their shadow can communicate with simplicity and strength. Two different realities collide in an image: a real world and a projected one. Shadows are graphically powerful and traditionally have sinister overtones. In film noir they are used with great drama to suggest entrapment or danger.

Shadowy art (opposite)
At first sight it appears that Tim Nobel and Sue Webster are just making a mess as they pile up debris found on the street on the highly polished floors of leading art galleries. Magically, once illuminated with a spotlight these seemingly random heaps of trash create perfectly formed shadows of the artists on the gallery wall. This witty 2002 self-portrait is made complete with the punning title – *Real Life Is Rubbish*. *See* Puns.

Shadowy satire (below)
Nineteenth-century satirist J. J. Grandville uses shadows to suggest the true nature of the politicians, public figures and the clergy depicted in this drawing – their shadows reveal the devil, bottles and decanters symbolizing drunkenness, the moon symbol of lunacy and a monkey symbolizing stupidity. *See* Caricature, Symbols.

Haunting shadows (right)
London DJ duo The Broken Hearts reveal their haunting side in this photo by Ian Bonhole, illustration by Rob Flowers. *See* www.robflowers.co.uk

La Caricature. *(Journal.)* Pl.3.

LES OMBRES PORTÉES.
(Planche. 1.)

Shigeo Fukuda, *Sea Cannot Be Cut Apart,* 1988
Artist and designer Shigeo Fukuda welded 2,084 pairs of scissors together to create the shape that casts this amazing shadow image of a galleon. *See* Illusion.

吸烟有害健康 **unicef**
联合国儿童基金会

A gun to his head (above)
Dad's smoking shadow holds a gun to the head of his child in this brilliant Chinese anti-smoking campaign. *See* Expressions Visualised.

Benson & Hedges ad (left)
An intriguing, award-winning and much discussed 1978 campaign for Benson & Hedges shot by legendary photographer Brian Duffy. At the time UK advertisers had been banned from showing people smoking or even from showing cigarettes. *See* www.duffyphotographer.com

DIY
Use shadows to reveal your ideas.

Brainjack
When a surprising or revealing shadow is cast it defies the viewer's mental expectations: a tension is created between the subject and its unexpected projection.

Further viewing
See the magic illusions created in shadow puppet theatres. *See* One thing looks like another.

Shock

Shock shouts louder than anything else in the visual cacophony of the street. Shock startles. It creates debate and challenges what can and can't be shown publicly. Many shocking advertising campaigns are banned by government watchdogs, provoking media coverage that further spreads the message; they make news.

'For photographs to accuse, and possibly to alter conduct, they must shock.'

Susan Sontag, writer

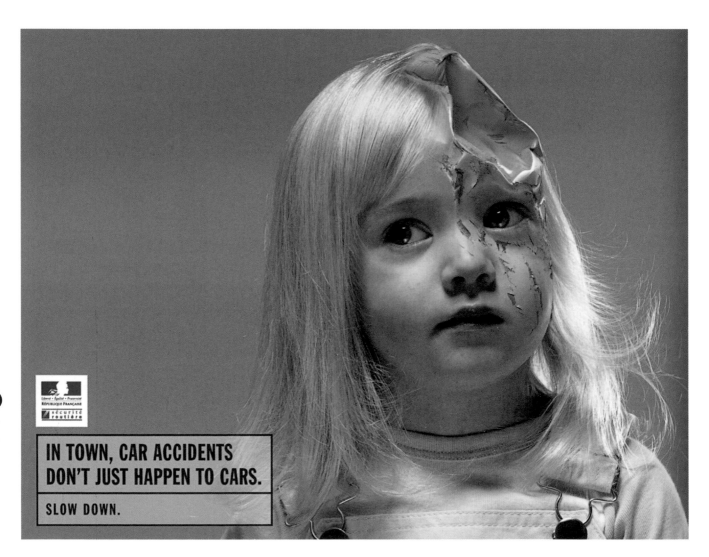

IN TOWN, CAR ACCIDENTS DON'T JUST HAPPEN TO CARS.

SLOW DOWN.

'We need to be shocked out of our complacency, out of our suburban lawns and swimming pools, in order to understand what's going on.'

Tibor Kalman, designer

Road safety poster (opposite)
This highly emotive image was created for Sécurité Routière, the French Road Safety Institute. It echoes the 1936 photo of a child killed by bombing used in the poster from the Spanish Civil War titled *If You Tolerate this Your Children Will Be Next*, that has become one of the most famous propaganda posters of all time.

Barnado's ad (below left)
One of a series of incredibly hard-hitting ads created for the charity Barnardo's, illustrating what could happen to abused or disadvantaged children without help. The Committee of Advertising Practice were so shocked that they had issued notices to newspapers and publications advising them not to run them. The editor of *The Guardian* newspaper ran the ad, responding: 'It is shocking but it is the sort of image that *Guardian* readers are sophisticated enough to deal with, and understand its message.'

Aphex Twin CD cover, 1999 (below right)
Shock, laced with dark and knowing humour permeate the work of director, video artist and photographer Chris Cunningham who created this sleeve for Aphex Twin in 1999. See his remarkable 2005 short movie *Rubber Johnny*.

Pulp, *This Is Hardcore*, album cover, 1998 (bottom right)
Wishing to shed their image as purveyors of wimpy art school pop, the band Pulp turned to art director Peter Saville – *see* Secret Messages – and artist John Currin to create the sleeve for a new CD. The cover they created caused storms of complaints and loads of publicity for taking its visual style, and its title, from the tawdry, abusive world of pornography.

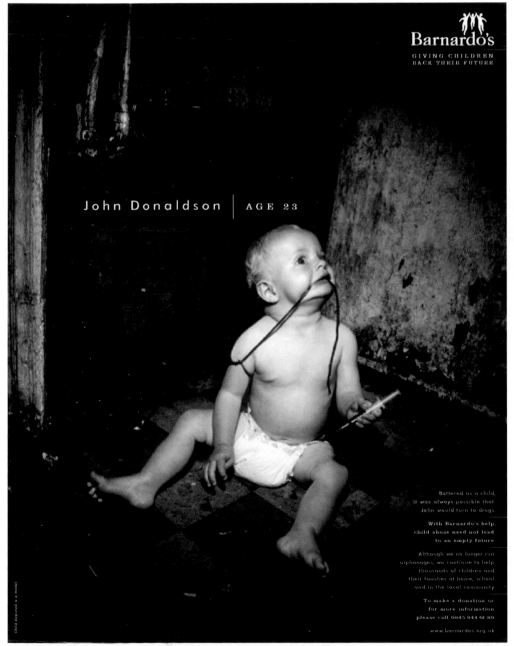

Barnardo's
GIVING CHILDREN
BACK THEIR FUTURE

John Donaldson | AGE 23

Battered as a child,
it was always possible that
John would turn to drugs.

With Barnardo's help,
child abuse need not lead
to an empty future.

Although we no longer run
orphanages, we continue to help
thousands of children and
their families at home, school
and in the local community.

To make a donation or
for more information
please call 0845 844 01 80.

www.barnardos.org.uk

DIY
Give your viewers shock treatments.

Brainjack
Shock urgently claims attention, penetrates our defences and fires our emotions. It is disarming and uncomfortable; it calls for action. It can ask questions that the viewer feels compelled to answer – it can demand collaboration. Real shock is unstoppable and disturbing; by creating visual nausea it can stir up emotions and touch hearts.

Signs

Signs condense and simplify messages and information in a pictorial form that is absorbed more quickly than the written word. By relying on visual imagery, they can bypass language barriers and be universally understood. The meanings and commands of signs are imprinted on our minds – we must actively learn road signage in order to drive legally. Signs are serious.

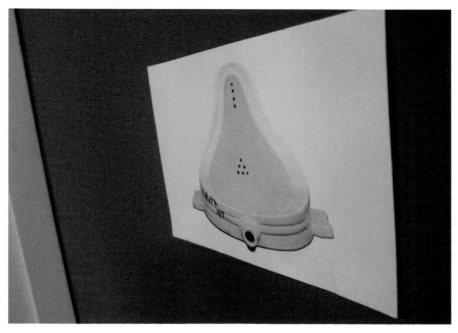

Road codes

In the United Kingdom the Highway Code simplifies the information conveyed by road signs and must be learnt by all drivers. The signs generally feature two codes; one uses different shapes of sign and the other uses colours. Circles indicate prohibited or restrictive signs while triangular signs are warnings. A red frame is used to express a command or hazard while a blue one represents additional information.

The language of signs

Signs command, warn, direct and instruct. They can advertise, aid navigation on foot and by transport and can contribute to the individuality of a city or place. Signs can be humorous – the Gents in an art gallery is indicated by Marcel Duchamp's famous urinal (opposite bottom left). They can be friendly (below left centre), can intrigue (opposite centre), be sources of humour and their messages can be subverted (below right). Signs can even be the source of new signs as in the example created for an Amsterdam bike store (opposite top).

DIY
Be playful with the language and conventions of signage.

Brainjack
They are the voice of authority – they give orders which, if disobeyed, can lead to arrest – so when they are used in an unexpected or subversive way the results are memorable.

Silhouettes

The sharp edges and flat blackness of traditional and historical hand-cut silhouettes make them highly graphic, simple, clear and pure images. Their flatness and sharpness mean objects of varying scales can be convincingly combined and juxtaposed. They are a magical visual language.

Rob Ryan, *Ladderkiss*
This intricate hand-cut silhouette by Cypriot-born artist Rob Ryan wonderfully combines figures, birds, clouds and leaves of different scales to create a magical world. *See* www.ryantownshop.blogspot.com

A visual language

Before the birth of photography hand-cut silhouettes were an inexpensive form of portrait. The subject was always seen in profile since this allowed more of the sitter's unique features be shown than would be visible in a full-face view. This established convention is part of the strength of silhouettes, in which the world is seen 'flat on' in a way we never usually choose to view it. The profile view is revealing, as can be seen in the work of Ruben Toledo whose silhouettes of women's fashions through the ages show the changing shapes of clothes and bodies.

Silhouettes of young people dancing were used for the global launch of the Apple iPod. The features, clothes, age and ethnicity of the models were unseen, allowing viewers to picture them only in their minds, where they could project their own thoughts about these details into the images.

Old silhouettes (above)
Two early nineteenth-century hand-cut silhouettes – popular, inexpensive portraits prior to the birth of photography.

New silhouette (left)
A street artist in China cuts the author's silhouette.

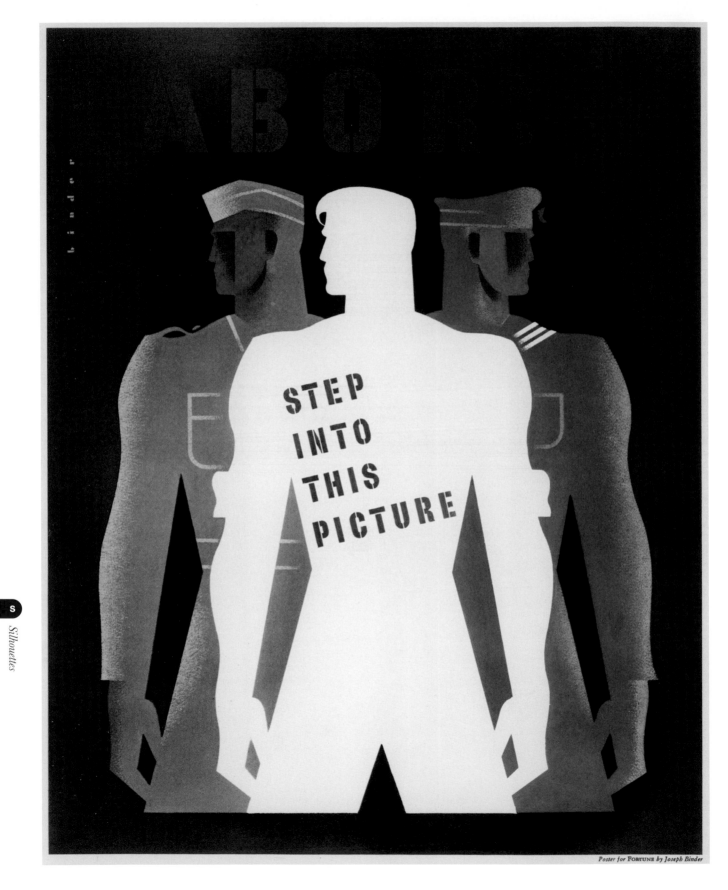

Poster for FORTUNE by Joseph Binder

Silhou-wit (above)
Silhou-wit displayed on a bathroom door.

Art silhouettes (left)
In this intriguing art installation newspapers from which every human figure featured in the news stories had been cut out and removed were stuck over the gallery windows. Viewers found the silhouettes created by the missing people filled with the city outside.

Labor poster (opposite)
Every American worker is represented by the silhouette in this World War II propaganda poster highlighting the contribution to the war effort made by the working man. It was designed in 1943 by Joseph Binder.

DIY
Explore the possibilities of silhouettes. Those of most objects are powerful. Outfits, props and backgrounds of the greatest opulence can be convincingly created with a zero budget through the imaginative use of scissors and paper or card. *See* Garage genius.

Brainjack
When figures and objects are seen only in silhouette they are not fully revealed; they are incomplete. This demands the viewers involvement to mentally 'fill in' what is unseen in the imagination.

Further viewing
See also Chinese paper-cutting, which offers a parallel visual language of exciting possibilities, and the paper silhouettes cut by the French artist Matisse.

Sketchbooks and scrapbooks

Every creative person keeps sketchbooks, scrapbooks or notebooks as a personal record of events, thoughts, half-formed ideas and things found or observed. They can be the focus for finding new connections and forming associations between unrelated materials and ideas. Sketchbooks and scrapbooks can act as part of the creative process, both for developing, collaging and connecting ideas and as an ideas bank: a constantly available store of memories, adventures, collections, souvenirs, experiences and thoughts. See You! (put yourself in it).

London sketchbook (above)
A collage of images of Piccadilly Circus on the inside cover of a London student's sketchbook.

Art student sketchbooks and notebooks (opposite)
Sketchbooks and notebooks can help form and focus ideas, record thoughts and experiences. Collecting images in sketchbooks can reveal unthought-of interrelationships.

'*We are constantly getting magazines, getting books and collecting images in sketchbooks.*'
Alan Aboud, art director

'I'm a hunter-gatherer. I've set up a system to electronically drag images into a scrapbook on my computer. I collect things that make you double-take.'

Georg Thesman, art director

'When researching on the internet you can see millions of fantastic things, but it's hard to see them simultaneously. Putting inspiring things you've found into a sketchbook and seeing them together allows you to see new opportunities for combinations that can form ideas.'

Ross Cooper, multidisciplinary designer

'I used to use scraps of paper to write down my ideas but I kept losing them. Sketchbooks are better, but sometimes these can become too precious. I now use really cheap ones.'

Jon Gledstone, art director

'For me a scrapbook is like a visual development diary, a personal journey. I use them for visual reference and creative development… I think making scrapbooks creates confidence in your visual language. When you're actually working on them, sticking things down, you explore space, tension and composition.'

Chris Priest, typographer

DIY
Keep sketchbooks, scrapbooks and notebooks. Use them to collect thoughts, memories, ideas, images and things that inspire you. Create a cut and pasted storehouse of ideas.

See the sketchbooks, scrapbooks and notebooks of your ideas heroes. Sketchbooks by Picasso, Peter Beard, Tim Walker and Cecil Beaton reveal their individual creative thinking.

Brainjack
Ideas from sketchbooks, notebooks and scrapbooks can offer maximum-strength communication when they have been digested and refined for months or even years until at maximum potency.

So bad
it's good

Our assessment of the creative worth of images and objects is based on our tastes. As we judge what we see, our internal taste barometer rises and falls between good and bad taste. Kitsch, trash and cheesy images fall firmly into the latter category. Though often dismissed as tacky, vulgar or simply awful, these images retain a special place in the hearts of many creative people – guilty pleasures that possess a potent and joyous 'so bad it's good' quality.

Pierre et Gilles, *Medusa,***1990 (right)**
Photographers Pierre et Gilles 1990
picture *Medusa* echoes the colouring
and composition of Tretchikoff
(see opposite).

Kitsch classics
Flying plaster ducks, *The Green Lady,*
garden gnomes, souvenir snow domes.

Kitsch heroes
Barbara Cartland, Jeff Koons,
Liberace, Jayne Mansfield, Vladimir
Tretchikoff, Andy Williams.

Great trash movies
Roger Corman made trashy films
about bikers, hippies, creatures from
beyond the grave and monsters from
outer space. His trash classics include
*Swamp Woman, The Trip, The Wild
Angels* and *Attack of the Crab Monsters.*
See also *Village of the Giants,* whose
publicity reads 'Teenagers zoom to
supersize and terrorize a town', and
Russ Meyer's *Faster Pussycat, Kill… Kill!*

The delight of kitsch

The self-taught Russian-born artist Vladimir Tretchikoff created paintings that, in print form, sold more copies than prints of van Gogh's *Sunflowers* or Leonardo da Vinci's *Mona Lisa*. The paintings drip with sentimentality; they show tearful children, blind beggars and ballerinas morphing into swans, all in a sickly, nauseous palette of colour. His *Chinese Girl*, known popularly as '*The Green Lady*', once hung in millions of suburban homes. Tretchikoff's magnificently awful paintings have been an inspiration for work by photographers Pierre et Gilles, and designer Wayne Hemingway.

Guilty pleasures

Kitsch has made Jeff Koons one of the richest artists in the world. He has single-handedly taken it from the walls, mantelpieces and sideboards of suburbia to the sophisticated surroundings of leading art galleries and the homes of wealthy collectors. Inspired by cheap souvenirs in tourist-trap gift shops, Koons – hailed as 'the king of kitsch' – exhibits massive sculptures of the Pink Panther cuddling a Playboy model accessorized with cheap gilt jewellery, a giant bear in a stripy coloured T-shirt asking a cheery British policeman for directions, and three cherubic angels pushing a pig.

At home with kitsch (above)
Designer Wayne Hemingway is so fond of Tretchikoff's paintings he had one enlarged to fill an entire wall of his home. Photo by Beth Evans. *See* www.vladimirtretchikoff.com

Paul Smith, Mills & Boon (right)
A memorable Paul Smith campaign features kitsch cover illustrations from schmaltzy Mills & Boon paperbacks.

Koons' masterpiece is a life-size white porcelain sculpture of Michael Jackson cuddling his pet chimp, Bubbles. Dressed in matching bandsman's outfits, they sit on scattered flowers, their hair and eyebrows highlighted in gold, their lips picked out in vivid red. It's magnificently shocking. A triumph of repulsive trashy tastelessness.

In on the joke
Part of the delight of kitsch is trying to guess the makers' motives: were they or weren't they deliberately creating tasteless work? Are they joking? Tretchikoff always thought of himself a a serious painter while Pierre et Gilles' tongues are firmly in their cheeks. Jeff Koons has always maintained publicly that his work is deadly serious – honestly.

The delight of cheese
Things that display great tastelessness are sometimes described as cheesy. Like kitsch, the lack of taste can be wholly unintentional on the part of the creators. Lionel Richie's music video *Hello* is a memorable cheese classic as is Bruce Springsteen's video for *Dancing in the Dark* – its catalogue of cheesiness was saluted by writer Sarfraz Manzoor for featuring 'terrible dad dancing, an indiscriminate usage of denim and camerawork that includes a shot beginning at Springsteen's feet and moving upwards, pausing with a tight shot of his crotch'. Both *Hello* and *Dancing in the Dark* stick in the mind far longer than numerous tasteful videos.

Television pop programmes of earlier decades often featured memorable cheese, created when bands and singers were asked to perform in front of inexpensively produced sets created by the show's designers. The Doors could be seen performing in front of a set made of hundreds of front doors and Petula Clark sang 'Sign of the Times' in front of a collection of road signs.

Some images that once would hardly have registered on the taste barometer mature to become cheesy; examples are photographs of trendy 1970s haircuts and fashion, and 1950s visions of future lifestyles. Such images have inspired photographers including David LaChapelle.

The language of trash
In the 1950s, posters that advertised films aimed at teenagers and the covers designed for cheap crime paperbacks began to exhibit a new visual and verbal language: trash. Lurid images, provocative poses and throbbing colours coupled with sensational titles, exaggerated claims and far-fetched plots are the DNA of trash, which promises titillation, quick thrills and violence.

Trash fan Quentin Tarantino caught its spirit magnificently in *Pulp Fiction* – a cocktail of burgers, sex, menace, sadism, brutal cartoonish violence, relentless garish colour, chopper motorbikes, open-top Cadillacs, throbbing music, drug abuse and overdoses, Marilyn lookalikes, pony tails, dwarfs and coffee-drinking. Its rapid-fire dialogue is laced with wit and obscenity.

Philippe Starck mines kitsch
As ruddy-cheeked garden gnomes mine the depths of bad taste, followers of the career of chic product designer Philippe Starck – known for his sleek, stylized and streamlined objects – didn't all get the joke when he created these very funny stools.

Nerd fashion
Photographer David Abrahams shot this
so bad its great 'nerdy fashion' story, styling
his models as geeks and posing and
lighting them to create what look like toxically
coloured high school portraits. *See* Movies,
www.davidabrahams.co.uk

DIY
Explore the full taste range.

Brainjack
Kitsch, cheese and trash
provoke a highly memorable,
jaw-dropping response from
viewers – that the creator
could not possibly be serious.

Surprise

Surprise is powerful. Surprising ideas can make people sit up and take notice. As art critic Waldemar Januszczak has written 'the role of art is to conjure up fresh experiences by hijacking the senses and surprising them'.

'What separates a brilliant idea from the pedestrian pack is the element of surprise.'
George Lois, designer

Diego Paccagnella, *Surprise Milan*, 2005
Surprise Milan did just that. Italian designer Diego Paccagnella created this project to promote Italian furniture company LAGO during Salone del Mobile, the worlds biggest design fair. The idea was to make Lago present in the streets with a living installation, for a week the five coloured cubes moved around the hot spots of Milan occasionally halting to create silent, enigmatic sculptures.

 DIY
Create messages that are revealed in surprising ways. For example, a message might appear inside a bar of soap when the intended recipient is washing; it could become visible at the bottom of a cup when someone finishes drinking their coffee – or be seen by others when the cup is raised. Or a message might be revealed when a condom is put on. *See* Unexpected venues.

 Brainjack
Because surprise occurs unexpectedly it can cause sudden feelings of wonder and amazement. It can communicate by upsetting the regular pattern of our lives.

Symbols

A symbol is something that can be used to visually represent something else. A heart is a symbol of love, a dove represents peace, scales symbolize justice and a skull stands for death. These simple symbols are used to denote complex concepts and are universally understood. The nature of the object used as a symbol often relates directly to what it symbolizes: our hearts pound when we are in love, doves are peaceful birds, scales can be seen as weighing right against wrong, and the very old and dying become skull-like.

Motivational carrot (above)
A carrot is a common symbol for a reward – possibly from the figure of speech 'carrot or stick' referring to the choice of offering a reward or a punishment to induce a result. For this 1979 paperback cover designer Derek Birdsall uses one to neatly communicate the subject of the book – motivation and incentives in business.

Skull *Judge* magazine, 1894 (right)
The skull – a symbol of death – is created by the boozy plotting of President Cleveland and Congressman Wilson in this 1894 cover illustration by Bernhard Gillam.

When Brenda Rawnsley was visiting artists around Europe in the late 1940s to commission posters for schools she met Picasso. She recalled: 'He did a drawing for me, then added a special symbol that meant he liked me. I think it's called a phallic symbol!'

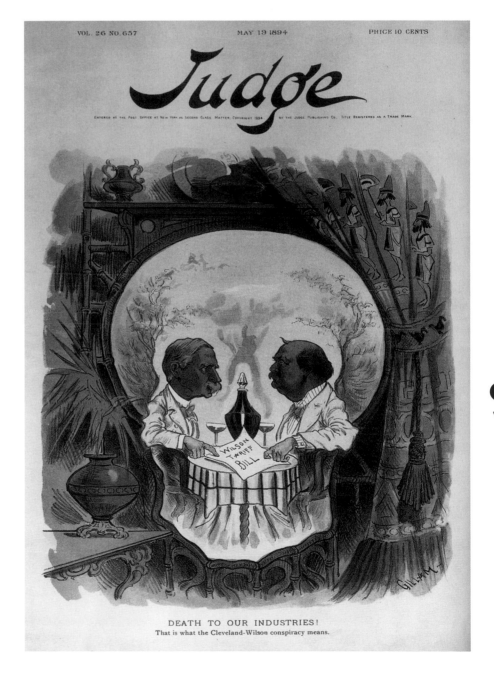

Animal symbols

The meaning and impact of individual symbols can change over time as new ones evolve and others slip out of use. A menagerie of birds and beasts was once used in classical paintings and the symbolism of some animals – like the owl (wisdom), the phoenix (regeneration), the lion (power and strength), the fox (cunning) and the dog (loyalty) – is still understood, while the frog as a symbol of slippery Satan is no longer recognized.

Animals symbolize countries and continents: the eagle for the United States and Mexico, the bear for Russia, the koala bear or kangaroo for Australia, the cockerel for France, the lion for Britain and the bull for Spain. These symbols are used in political cartoons.

The Greyhound bus was once a key symbol of America. It expressed the romance of travel and was seen in movies, art, design and popular music. With the decline of this form of transport its symbolic importance has waned.

Flower symbols

Native flowers and plants are national symbols: the thistle represents Scotland, the daffodil Wales, the rose England and the tulip Holland. The four-leaf clover is well known for symbolizing good luck.

Fruit and vegetable symbols

Fruit has symbolic potency; the apple stands for knowledge and temptation, as in the Bible and religious paintings, and can also symbolize a gift for a teacher, New York City and the discovery of gravity. The apple was also used by the Beatles for their record company and by Apple Computers. Cherries are a symbol of virginity, and life has been called 'a bowl of cherries'. Tangerines can symbolize Christmas and sliced oranges amateur sport, while in the United States a lemon is a car that constantly breaks down. In France a pear can represent a dull person (*see* One thing looks like another) and going pear-shaped means something has gone wrong. A carrot stands for a reward – a stick is its opposite – and also the ability to see in the dark. A leek is another symbol of Wales while a gooseberry is an unwanted third person on a date.

Local symbols

Some symbols have purely local significance. For example, in the United Kingdom only football fans understand that a prawn sandwich represents the recent corporatization and sanitization of live games. Only in America is a straw boater thrown in the air a symbol of political success, while only the Chinese understand that a green hat symbolizes a man with a cheating partner.

The Unteachables
problem kids, progressive solutions
New series starts Tuesday 9.00pm

Common symbols
Black armband = mourning
Black leather jacket = rebellion
White feather = cowardice
Cigar = success, wealth or birth of a child
Champagne = celebration
● *Red dot = painting sold*
★ *Gold star = praise from a teacher*
Books = an educated person
Burnt book = a society in trouble
Burning cross = beware mad racists
Wooden spoon = last place in a contest / failure
Empty bird cage with open door = freedom / escape
Screwed up ball of paper = a rejected idea
Chrysalis = potential for a beautiful outcome
White picket fence = the American Dream / comfortable success
Olive branch = offer of peace
Emptying hourglass = time is running out

Chinese symbols

As in Western visual culture, creatures and other natural forms dominate Chinese symbolism. The fish – a biblical symbol of belief in Christianity – is a symbol of wealth in China. This is because the Chinese word for fish is identical to that for abundance and affluence. The peach symbolizes longevity and immortality. The tiger represents courage and bravery, and has the power to drive away demons. This is perhaps the origin of the expression 'paper tiger', which describes a person or country that appears to be powerful but is in fact ineffectual and weak.

Architectural symbols

In architecture the classical pillars of town halls and banks are symbols of wisdom and experience. Because these buildings in our high streets remind us of those created by the founders of modern civilization, the ancient Greeks and Romans, they tell us visually that the occupants have authority and knowledge, and that we can trust them – though whether we can or not is open to debate.

The Empire State Building in New York, the Eiffel Tower in Paris, the onion-domed churches of Red Square in Moscow, Sydney Opera House, the Colosseum in Rome, and the London Eye symbolize the excitement of the cities where they stand. It is too soon to tell whether the 'sail' building in Dubai, which was deliberately built in an attempt to create an exciting symbol for the city, will come to represent excitement or a city built on sand.

The skeletal last building left standing after the bombing of Hiroshima in 1945 has become symbolic of far more than a Japanese city: in the minds of millions of people it stands for the wanton slaughter of innocent people and the evils of nuclear warfare.

Symbols in business

Companies attempt to distil their ethos into symbols. The Nike tick is a successful example: its simple graphic form delivers a positive message of success and implies swiftness. *See* Expressions visualized.

The Unteachables (opposite)
An apple can symbolize many different things – here it is used to denote a gift to a teacher from a pupil, the X-ray revealing that it bears a deadly secret. *See* X-rays.

Seven deadly sins (left)
A mixture of old and new symbols are used to illustrate a series of articles on the sinfulness of professional footballers. The backstabbing dagger is a symbol that goes back to Brutus in ancient Rome, while the computer games handset smartly symbolizes early twenty-first century indolence. The takeaway meat pie used to represent gluttony has its source as a symbol in the popular football terrace chant directed at all plump footballers – 'who ate all the pies?'

DIY
Find, collect and create symbols. Learn by examining the huge range of symbols that have been used in everyday communication, design, advertising, movies and art. Look at the ones used in other cultures; for example, Chinese symbols are fascinating and are so numerous they have been collected in bulging dictionaries.

Brainjack
Commonly used visual symbols communicate quickly as their meaning is clearly pre-established in viewers' minds.

A freshly created symbol communicates when the viewer makes the connection between it and the object or concept it is being used to symbolize. New symbols give viewers the mental reward and satisfaction gained from spotting and making this connection.

T

Tension between words and images

The content of magazines and newspapers, books, posters, websites and advertisements is a fusion of text and images. Sometimes images are dominant and are supported by the text, at other times the text predominates. Art also features interplay between the title and artwork. To communicate powerfully the relationship between images and text must be carefully considered. The most memorable communications feature a dynamic synergy between the two.

Paris girls (above)
The subtitles that appear on the screen during foreign movies often create dynamic fusions of words and image, as here in a still from Godard's *A Bout de Souffle*. *See* Movies, Fusion.

Simon Kavanagh, *My Mind's Eye*, installation, 2006 (opposite)
Words and images provocatively combine in this installation created by media artist Simon Kavanagh. Text and pictures are programmed to randomly merge on adjoining halves of the screen. Each word overprints an ever-changing selection of images of urban spaces, travel and culture. Eccentric concepts are created that clash, harmonize or bewilder. Kavanagh programmed this digitally projected work of art to never repeat the same combination of images and text. *See* Digitality, www.mediartists.info

Tension between words and images

Words people and image people

The creative partnership of words and images is replicated in the world of advertising where it is traditional for a visual person to be coupled with a words person. This works most successfully when, like the best meeting of words and images, there is great reverberation between the two.

'You see a picture in tension with words. The whole image is like two live electric cables: one is the picture, one is the words. The viewer grasps the cables, creating an electric shock and sparks in their head.'

Clive Challis , art director and teacher

'William Blake is the godfather of graphic design. He mixed his words and his images in a way that they were intersoluble, they were so integrated. He virtually invented graphic design in the way he worked.'

Ken Garland, designer

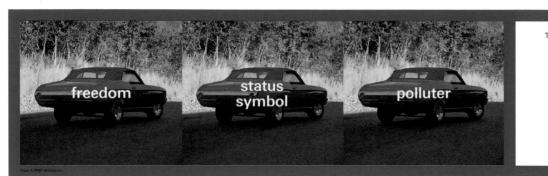

freedom   status symbol   polluter

The more you look at the world, the more you recognise that what one person values may be different to the next.

www.hsbc.com

HSBC
The world's local bank

THE BIG QUESTION:
IS ECONOMIC PROGRESS KILLING The PLANET?

Jonathan Barnbook / adbusters,
***The Big Question*, poster, 1999 (left)**
Multidisciplinary designer Jonathan Barnbrook creates a highly dynamic synergy between text and images in this poster commissioned by adbusters, the Canadian based anti-advertising bimonthly. Layers of type and images of disparate scales and forms interrelate, clash, overlap and harmonise to deliver a big question. The poster was produced to coincide with the 1999 World Trade Organization summit in Seattle. *See* www.barnbrook.net, www.adbusters.org, Making maps and Questions.

HSBC ad (above)
One of a great series of ads for the bank HSBC that construct a very smart tension between images and words with incredible simplicity. An image, repeated three times, each overprinted with a single word create three greatly differing choices of interpretation. Viewers are engaged by both appreciation of the often opposing meanings and by the challenge to make a personal choice of juxtaposition (*see* Juxtaposition).

 DIY
Balance the tension between images and words carefully and ensure they fuse powerfully.

Brainjack
In a great partnership words and images enrich each other. The two elements bounce off each other and rebound in the viewer's mind.

 Further viewing
See works by the American artists Duane Michals and Barbara Kruger which mix creative writing and creative photography.

T

Tension between words and images

Torn images

Tearing away a section of an image reveals an underlayer, and a comparison is created between it and the top layer. Something hidden is revealed or bursts into view.

Anti-war Uncle Sam
Personality Posters produced this searing anti-war poster (right) in 1972 during the Vietnam war, violently tearing into James Montgomery Flag's famous recruiting poster (above) that had been used to encouraged American volunteers to fight during both World War I and World War II. The ferocity of the tear adds further impact to the revelation that Uncle Sam – the personification of America – is underneath it all a symbol of death.

John Smith's beer ad (bottom)
In this very funny add for John Smith's beer, the wind appears to have torn away most of a billboard poster to reveal an old one beneath.

DIY
Use torn images to reveal hidden things.

Brainjack
Tearing is a physical and often destructive act. Rips and tears can be boldly graphic and communicate, powerfully, that they were created in anger or with urgency. An image with a tear can convey that the comparison between the layers is a secret or hidden truth.

Travel

The Globetrotter (below)
Photographer Nick Meers has criss-crossed the world with this suitcase, working on his spectacular travel books. Appropriately, the make of the case is a Globetrotter. *See* www.nickmeers.com

Images of China (opposite)
Travel inspires by revealing new colours, shapes and patterns, it can teach us new ways of thinking and new methods of creating and doing things. The author's images opposite show an old people's playground in China, a battery-operated mosquito killer that allows you to simultaneously kill the pests and practice your backhand, paper sun hats, and traditional Chinese clothes and fabric design.

Travel provides inspiration and insights by showing completely new ways of doing things. Looking at a snapshot of a group of women in Rajasthan in India, fashion designer Paul Smith reflected: 'It can easily inspire how I put my clothes together in a show, or how I might combine those colours in a shirt.'

Designer Ken Garland reflected on the power of travel: 'A new environment is stimulating; it's something you haven't witnessed before, it's a liberation. We take away in our mind's eye things that we don't digest at the time. When I first went to a strange environment I was 18; I went to Germany. The images that I absorbed then were only digested later, some of them decades later. When we travel, willy-nilly images are impregnated in us. We take them home and recover them in our mind's eye later. Among the most liberating places I have visited are Mexico and Bangladesh. I'm now working on books digesting the things I saw there years ago.'

Grand tourists

In the seventeenth, eighteenth and early nineteenth centuries wealthy English gentlemen travelled abroad on an educational 'gap year' known as the Grand Tour. They visited France, Italy and Greece, stopping in Paris, Venice, Rome and Athens. This experience changed the lives of many grand tourists, including painter J.M.W. Turner, poets Lord Byron and Percy Bysshe Shelley, and architects Inigo Jones and Robert Adam. They found creative inspiration for their work through immersion in a foreign culture – both high and low. For them travel was a creative rite of passage. Jones and Adam, for example, were inspired by the classical buildings they saw in Rome and Athens. They recycled elements of these, in numerous variations, in their designs for English country houses, churches and public buildings – they combined domes, columns, porticoes and façades in many different ways, using them as playfully as if they were massive pieces of Lego.

New ways
New and exciting ways of solving problems can be revealed by travel – for example how to transport loads of newspapers and how to take advantage of the concrete bollards sited outside your café.

DIY
Become an explorer: make voyages of discovery and find new territory. Be curious about the world; go out and see it. Embark on your own Grand Tour. Travel surprises, and can overwhelm the senses with new experiences. If you can't go to all the places you want to visit, be an explorer in your own country. Embrace the different nationalities and cultures on your doorstep.

You can also travel in your imagination. Check out the world film shelf in your local DVD store and experience visual culture from around the globe: be inspired by movies from India, South America, Africa, Japan and China. And perhaps the least expensive way to learn about the world is by visiting museums, reading and watching the news on television.

Brainjack
The mind-broadening capacity of travel has been long known.

Type

When words are used in visual communication it is vitally important to consider exactly how they will look to the viewer. The letterforms selected to spell words out in posters, websites, illustrations and advertisements bring additional meaning to the text.

Type is grouped in different typefaces, and letters are known as characters expressing the fact that different letterforms have different personalities. Like human faces, these can convey a variety of messages. Design teacher and writer Bo Bergstrom wrote that they 'can be pompous, pretentious, hesitant, tentative, cheeky, affected, harsh, cheap and vulgar. But they can also be open, lucid, clear, elegant, simple and distinguished.' The face you select needs to stand out in the crowd.

Nick Pride, *Bristol*, 2007 (below and bottom)
Pride creates huge collages from printed type and found objects describing his work as 'a record of the typography of everyday life, the ephemera that surrounds us and passes through our hands, often unnoticed.'

T-eye-pography (above)
A giant exclamation that passengers should keep an eye out. *See* Eyes.

Charlie Chaplin becomes typecast (right)
One of a series of ads for a Brazilian newspaper that use type to recreate images of famous people and events, it was created by agency DM9 DDB Publicidade in 1998.

Folha de S. Paulo. Há 77 anos retratando o mundo com palavras.

Typecasting

Choosing a typeface to express words in visual communication should be as carefully considered as selecting an actor to play a role in a theatre production or movie.

Autobiographical designs

Typefaces can be seen as being autobiographical. Some designers even name the ones they design after themselves. For example, Baskerville, Bodoni, Frutiger and Gill were created by John Baskerville, Giambattista Bodoni, Adrian Frutiger and Eric Gill. The text of this paragraph is set in ITC New Baskerville. What do you learn about the designers by looking at their letterforms?

Lettering in art

Lettering and type has been a source of inspiration and a tool for many artists, including Robyn Denny, Jasper Johns, Peter Blake and Barbara Kruger.

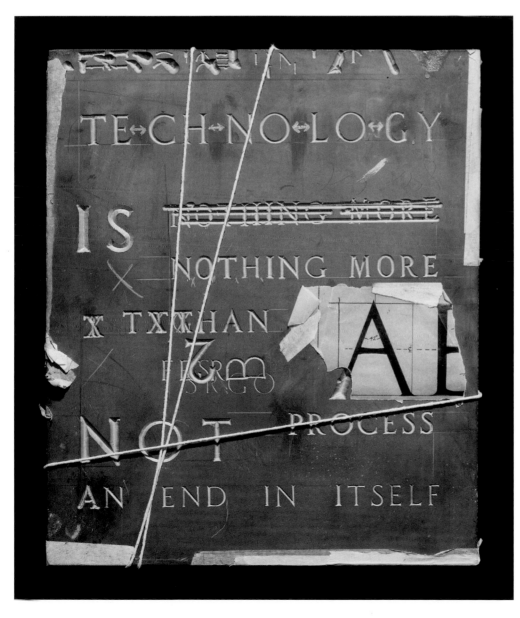

Jonathan Barnbrook, *Technology Is Nothing More Than a Process, Not an End in Itself*, 1990
Multidisciplinary designer Jonathan Barnbrook mixed technology and craft to create a series of typographic stone carvings using a machine normally used to produce inexpensive gravestones. He wrote 'the machine uses a primitive pantograph system, templates and a drill to create the letterforms. The quotes on the stones deal with issues of technology. I tried to produce carving with a vocabulary appropriate to the machine.' *See* www.barnbrook.net

 DIY
Love letters. Carefully consider the character you want to bring to the words in a message. Learn the typefaces that have been the 'face of each year' throughout the history of design and visual communication.

Collect impactful typography. Look at examples from other nations and cultures. Learn from the different ways they accentuate and add weight to communication. The different uses of punctuation marks in Spanish typography are an example.

Explore new and old ways of creating and printing words including calligraphy and letterpress.

Experiment with typography that complements the message you want to convey and with typography that clashes with it.

Finally, if type is 'the clothing words wear', Futura is the Little Black Dress.

 Brainjack
Typography can visually amplify the words it spells out, which makes for more vociferous communication in the minds of viewers.

T

Type

U

Unexpected venues

It is said that when trying to communicate, the only space worth buying is the space inside viewers' heads. The usual spaces purchased for spreading messages are billboards, posters, 30-second television and cinema advertisements, magazine and newspaper pages and space on the internet. As communication through these traditional slots becomes increasingly ineffective, new and unexpected spaces can be found that convey messages in different and more exciting ways.

Step up (top left)
Jimmy Turrell turned these airport steps into a massive ad for Kyocera. *See* www.jimmyturrell.com

Spaghetti source (top right)
Mondo Pasta's great 'noodleslurper' ad.

Squeeze box (above left)
To promote London's annual Camden Irish Music Festival, agency RKCR/Y&R London turned bendy buses into accordions.

New York transportation (above right)
New York subway riders boarding this train found themselves transported to another world – well, another continent – in this 2010 Dutch Tourist Board campaign.

Living stamp (opposite)
Workers in UK post offices become living postage stamps through this witty and unexpected use of the security glass at their counters. *See* Rescale.

Creative urban disturbances

The best creative interruptions to the usual flow of life can totally alter the viewer's mindset and how they think about the urban environment. When sculptor Antony Gormley positioned life-size sculptures on roofs in central London and New York they created an extraordinary, unsettled feeling among viewers: they seemed to be sinister figures watching passers-by, or snipers. Other artists, designers and advertising agencies have experimented with creative disturbances in cities, including wrapping buildings, trees, cars and sculptures in soft materials.

Painting the town

Attempts have been made to communicate speedily with an entire city using text cut into the treads of bicycle tyres. These were painted and wherever the cycle was pedalled the tyres printed the message on to the streets.

Projections

Still or moving images projected on to urban surfaces can turn them into massive canvases and screens. Public buildings, blocks of flats, storefronts, pavements, monuments and concrete flyovers have been creatively used as unexpected venues for projections. Their sheer

scale in the city environment – on surfaces far larger than most cinema screens – is instantly arresting. Projections have been used for advertising, social campaigning, celebrations and as art.

Projections can have great impact when they are used interactively. A Chinese design student created an anti-smoking campaign in which dying lungs were beamed directly on to cigarette smokers in college smoking areas. The projections were triggered by smoke censors every time someone lit up. *See* Digitality.

Mark Boyle and Joan Hills pioneered creative projections in the 1960s, working with underground psychedelic bands. They projected huge images of fizzing fluids, bubbling chemical reactions and slides left to liquefy in the heat of the projector. They thought of their projections, which were beamed on to the walls, ceiling and audience at concerts rather than the stage, as 'another instrument'. These techniques inspired the design of the multiprojector creative light shows of the late 1980s rave culture.

Shop window projections
Fashion designer Paul Smith pioneered the retail use of projections in his first shop in Nottingham in England,

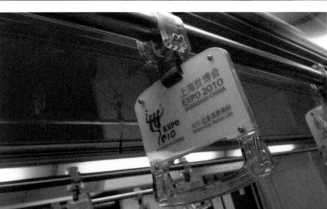

Unexpected communication barrier 1 (top left)
Spotted in London.

Unexpected communication barrier 2 (middle left)
Spotted in Shanghai.

Get a grip (left)
The grip on a tube train provides a handy place to advertise.

On the edge (top right)
The foredge of a magazine provides a new venue for ads.

Exhibition on track (above)
This exhibition of harrowing pictures of the effects of war and famine around the globe by photojournalist Tom Stoddard found a totally new audience when staged at Bristol Temple Meads station – passengers awaiting trains and those on board trains at the station could view the massive prints.

in the 1970s. He turned its window into a screen at night and used a carousel projector with a timer.

Taking a message to the people

The use of unexpected urban venues is nothing new. The Artists International Association put on an exhibition of war pictures in 1941 in London that attracted a staggering and unprecedented attendance of 150,000 people in three weeks. Rather than choosing a conventional venue such as a municipal art gallery they had staged the show in the ticket hall of a central London Underground station.

Think big

The bottled-water company Évian won consumers' hearts through the benevolent act of paying for the renovation of the much-loved though run-down Brixton Lido outdoor swimming pool in south London. As part of the refit the pool was repainted with the company's logo, creating a gigantic message that could be seen from passing planes. Everyone won with this idea: local people got a beautiful pool and Évian gained nationwide press coverage.

Palace projection (above)
Buckingham Palace was turned into a gigantic screen when multiple still and moving images were projected onto London landmarks as part of the celebrations of the sixtieth anniversary of the end of World War II.

Smashing time (right)
Windows provided the venue for this smashing Dutch ad.

On a carousel, Venice Airport (above)
When Italian agency Admcom turned the luggage carousel at Venice Marco Polo Airport into a spinning roulette wheel to advertise the Venice Casino it became the talk of magazines, online publications and creative blogs around the world.

Escalating ideas (left)
For many years ads have been positioned beside escalators for people to view as they ride up or down, here the escalator itself becomes a massive message carrier.

 DIY
Constantly be on the lookout for original and innovative venues for communication and new ways to disseminate images. Cities, towns and their streets are always changing and evolving. Be observant.

Consider using events, projections, installations, objects, clothing and sound to send messages.

 Brainjack
Using an unexpected venue for a message can instantly capture the audience's imagination and buy the space in their heads. Viewers of a traditionally placed message know you are trying to tell, or sell, something but in a new venue it sneaks up on them. A message that is received unexpectedly has a great chance of sticking.

V

Visual
metaphors

When someone moves house in Greece they hire a metaphor van: metaphor is Greek for removal and transportation. Visual metaphors transport meaning by making comparisons that reveal that something familiar possesses the qualities of something else. It is removed from its original context and transferred to another.

Ken Garland, *Celtic Knot*
Ken Garland wrote about finding visual metaphors in the street: 'I can rarely take a photograph without drawing a metaphor from it either at the time or subsequently. On a street leading down to the docks in Galway I photographed a piece of rope that had been run over by a truck. It was a beautiful Celtic knot that was a metaphor, for me, for things Irish. Subsequently I turned the photograph the other way and began to see it as a metaphor for the island of Ireland. The top of the knot became Northern Ireland linked to Southern Ireland, a very strong link as they are one island. I then saw the top of the knot as an unlit fuse which could explode all the island. The metaphor was complete. Although we've had lots of trouble in Ireland we've never had the complete conflagration that could have occurred.'

'A metaphor has the ability to simply encapsulate a far greater concept than first meets the eye.'
Ken Garland, designer

'Visual metaphors can nail really complex things and deliver them with huge simplicity.'
Schway Whar, designer

Metaphors in nature

There are numerous inspiring metaphors in nature. Seeds represent growth, buds represent future possibility, tree rings represent history or the passing of time, blooming flowers and rainbows represent creativity, while clouds can represent thoughts, dreams or ideas.

Metaphors in the movies

The designer Ken Garland described how film-makers have used metaphors in their work: 'The barn-raising scene in *Witness* is a metaphor for a society that is absolutely interdependent. The film-maker makes a contrast to the dislocated society that the hero has come from in the city. He is presented with a society that is totally integrated. As he joins to raise the barn he experiences our loss of a sense of community. The director Peter Weir knew about this; he was brought up in the country outside Sydney and used this experience. In *Citizen Kane* Orson Welles – who had lost the security of his parents and family home in childhood – uses the sledge 'Rosebud' as a metaphor for Charles Foster Kane's lost childhood; it's haunting.' *See* You! (put yourself in it).

The barn-raising scene is wonderfully parodied in *Kingpin*.

Partnership (above)
A great metaphor for partnership, spotted on the streets of Suzhou, China – the umbrella holder gets a lift while the cyclist gets shade – everybody wins!

China as a rollercoaster (left)
A metaphor for the new China: it's a thrilling ride – but its not quite joined up yet.

DIY
Examine and collect metaphors you find in movies, literature, photography and painting. Coin new metaphors.

Brainjack
Viewers think more creatively, in exciting and memorable ways when objects or concepts are removed from their natural environments to the more abstract and imaginative metaphorical world.

In his great book on creative advertising, *Hey Whipple, Squeeze This*, adman Luke Sullivan writes: 'Part of what makes metaphors in ads so effective is that they involve the reader. They use images already in the reader's mind, twist them to our message's purpose, and ask the reader to close the loop for us.'

Visual metaphors

W

Word of mouth

The word of mouth tour
Converse spurned traditional promotional methods to launch their trainers in China, instead sending rock 'n' roll bands out on a lightning tour, travelling with all their equipment on a bus. The excitement of the acts and the spontaneity of the events quickly spread the itinerary on the internet ensuring huge crowds at every stop.

Messages can be conveyed from person to person in addition to coming from billboards, television or the printed media. Advertising and marketing companies are increasingly exploring new grass-roots methods of communication.

Innovative street-level interruptions to our daily lives can provoke epidemics of word-of-mouth recommendations. To promote their products, advertisers have begun to experiment with street ambassadors and flash-mob events where public spaces are filled with crowds orchestrated through text messages, the internet or fliers.

illy world tour (this page and opposite)
In 2001 Italian coffee manufacturers illy were approached by two art students with an idea – they'd like to drive round the world in one of illy's iconic delivery vans, stopping where they pleased to hand out coffee to those they met. illy bravely said OK, and supported the project. One of the students Diego Paccagnella commented 'they wanted to see what happened. Most people in industry want to know from A to Z exactly what you are going to do. Surprises are not allowed [see Paccagnella's later *Surprise Milan* project in Surprise]. But illy wanted that unpredictability." The pair set off in a 50cc Piaggio Ape van with an espresso machine in the back, a foldable tent on top and huge numbers of disposable coffee cups. Not allowed to drive on the motorway in such a tiny van they meandered along, stopping in places not even on the map. Visiting town squares, historic places, art schools and calling in on interesting people on the way – they arrived unannounced at the studios of Dutch design group Droog in Amsterdam (see Counter-intuition), pressing the bell and simply saying 'the coffee's arrived, come down!' The trip became a social experiment, using coffee as a catalyst for conversation and human interaction – 'some people loved the idea straight away, laughing and getting into it: others just stood in amazement,' said Paccagnella. This innovative adventure is in the memories of the numerous people encountered en route, whose lives were pleasantly interrupted by a spontaneous coffee break, gossip of which was sure to spread.

King Mob flash-mob

Flash-mobbing was inspired by events organized by followers of the Situationist International, a political art movement, in the 1960s. Its London group, known as King Mob, created mass mingles in which its members and their friends filled public spaces unannounced. In one of these events they crammed into the toy section of Selfridges department store and gave the toys to passing children.

Global gossip

We pass on gossip, rumours and great jokes we've heard to our friends. It's human nature to retell stories. The venues for jokes and gossip were once the office water-cooler, the pub, canteen, café or street corner. Now, in addition to this face-to-face communication, the internet provides numerous avenues for spreading the word about new things.

Cadbury's Gorilla and 'eyebrows' advertisements gained huge audiences beyond their television slots when they spread further via the internet. They were the first advertisements to enjoy the benefits of global gossip power when numerous parodies were uploaded within days of their launch. Hundreds of thousands of versions of the soundtracks were downloaded as ring tones.

Viewers have always talked about the advertisements they love and repeated catchphrases from their favourites – the 'Whassup!' greeting from the United Kingdom Budweiser campaign spread like wildfire – and the internet now enables them to edit and spoof, then upload, these, giving the advertiser the benefit of far more exposure at no extra cost.

 DIY
Create messages that entertain in a gossip-worthy way. Provide grist for the internet rumour mill.

Collect urban myths – those bizarre and untrue stories that circulate through retelling, things that happened to a friend of a friend. Try connecting your ideas to well-known examples of these myths. Artist John Baldessari created a series of images of ice cubes with words concealed inside them; his inspiration was an urban myth sweeping America that a cola manufacturer had concealed images of naked, copulating couples within the ice cubes in their advertisements.

 Brainjack
It is human nature to find pleasure in being the first to know about something new, funny, interesting or secret. The desire to share this knowledge with friends follows naturally.

Wordplay

Smirnoff see-through small ads (below)
Hidden agendas are revealed in this witty
advert that uses the acronyms and unique
language of the Lonely Hearts ad, created
by agency Lowe Howard Spink in 1997.

Economist bus (right)
This ad for the business journal *The
Economist* appeared on the top of London
buses in 1990. A wonderful idea delivered
with perfect wordplay that sends the
message that purchasers of the magazine
achieve great career success. It was
created by agency Abbott Mead Vickers.
See Unexpected venues.

Be inspired by words. Engage with the joy, fun and exuberance of words and wordplay in your work.

The success of two celebrated advertisements – Labour Isn't Working and Hallo Boys – hinged on wordplay that exploited different meanings of the same words.

The Labour Isn't Working poster was designed to attack Britain's Labour Party and was created for its arch rivals, the Conservatives, by the advertising agency Saatchi & Saatchi. It pivots on the double meaning of 'labour '– used here to mean both the political party and the workers who were unemployed. Writer Anthony Howard described the advertisement as 'the most powerful poster in post-war politics'.

In the Hallo Boys advertisement for Wonderbra, the two words greet both male admirers and a new-found cleavage.

Collecting words
Adman Leo Burnett collected
memorable wordplay to use in his
work: 'not maxims, gags or slang
in its ordinary sense, but words,
phrases and analogies that convey
a feeling of sod-buster honesty and
drive home a point. I sometimes run
across these phrases in a newspaper
story or in a chance conversation.'

Great new words
Presenteeism: the presence in the
workplace of individuals who, while
they appear to be at work, spend
their days surfing the internet,
social networking and sending
and receiving personal emails.
Presenteeism, like absenteeism, is
a huge frustration to employers.
Cyberia: the place where people
who don't use the internet live.
Volcation: the extra period of holiday
in April 2010 caused by aircraft in
the UK being grounded because an
Icelandic volcano had erupted.

Economy with words

It is important to handle words carefully and weigh up each one to decide whether it should be used in a design. Hallo Boys and Labour Isn't Working use just two and three words respectively.

When telegrams were a form of mass communication hand delivered by the postal service in tiny envelopes and used to send urgent messages of good or bad news there was a charge for each word and the messages were therefore brief and succinct. The explorer Captain Scott received one that consisted of just seven words from his arch rival: BEG LEAVE INFORM YOU PROCCEEDING ANTARCTIC AMUNDSEN. Writer Adam Nicolson commented that, 'In seven exquisitely courteous words, the bottom falls out of a man's life.' In the film *Cabaret*, Sally Bowles says that if her mean father heard she had leprosy his telegram would read: GEE KID TOUGH. SINCERELY HOPE NOSE DOESN'T FALL OFF. LOVE as he knew there would be extra charge after ten words.

DIY
Collect words, quotes, slang, patois, jargon, overheard small talk and slips of the tongue.

Examine different ways of using words and language; every social group has its own vernacular. Study newspaper headlines, pop songs, poetry and text messages, all of which use words, expressions, phrases and grammar very differently.

Imagine you have to pay for every word you use, then find the most economical way to send your message.

Become a wordsmith. If the words you are seeking don't exist, create new ones and fuse old ones together. Search for words hidden within words.

Brainjack
Play is pleasurable. Carefully created wordplay and games with words can engage viewers and fill their minds with joy.

Further viewing
See the Two Ronnie's 'four candles/fork handles' sketch on YouTube for brilliant wordplay. *See* Puns.

Treasure houses of words
Explore words using dictionaries and a thesaurus (the word means treasure) that lists words with related meanings.

All reference books can be wonderful treasure houses with much to explore. They can take you off at tangents and on exciting journeys: searching for one piece of information leads to finding another.

Alternatively, get lost in a reference book and find things by mistake. Follow all the leads in cross-references and footnotes – they will take you on unexpected adventures that can lead to inspiration. Become lost in the treasure houses.

Jonathan Barnbrook, *Designers, stay away from corporations that want you to lie for them*, **billboard, 2000**
Multidisciplinary designer Barnbrook is a passionate advocate of the ability of designers to effect change through their work and he is highly active in political and social causes. He created this billboard using a quote from designer Tibor Kalman (*see* Making faces) to provocatively convey a call for more meaningful design. The billboard was unveiled to coincide with an American Institute of Graphic Arts conference. *See* www.barnbrook.net

'Champagne for my real friends and real pain for my sham friends.'
Traditional drinking toast

X

X-rays

X-rays are used for medical and security purposes to reveal what the eye cannot see. This element of revelation can be used creatively. Artists, designers and cartoonists have used X-rays image to depict people's inner thoughts and hidden facets; photographer Helmut Newton used them to create stunning fashion pictures of luxury shoes and jewellery. Beautiful X-rays have also revealed the amazing inner structures of plants and shells.

John Heartfield, *Adolf, the Superman Swallows Gold and Talks Tinplate,* **1932**
In the 1930s German artist Helmut Herzfeld aka John Heartfield made numerous attacks on the Nazi party using photomontage as his weapon. In this poster created for the 1932 elections he used an X-ray superimposed onto a photo of Hitler in the midst of making a speech to reveal the Nazi leader as a hollow, spineless automaton supported by piles of gold from his plutocrat backers, his speech is garbage – the tinplate of the title is German slang for junk.

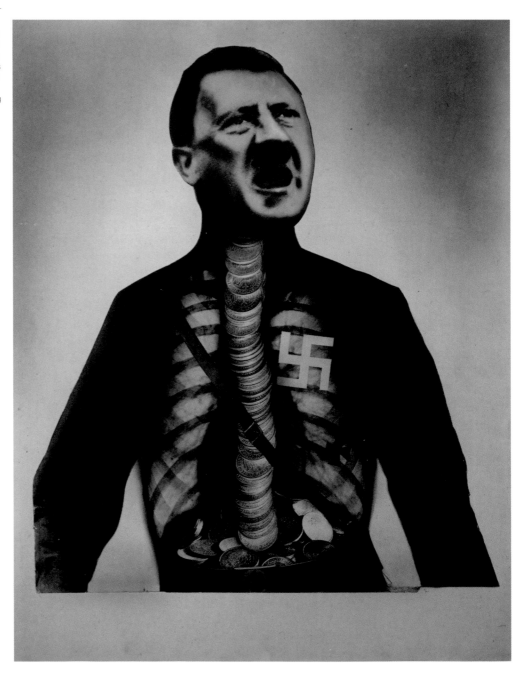

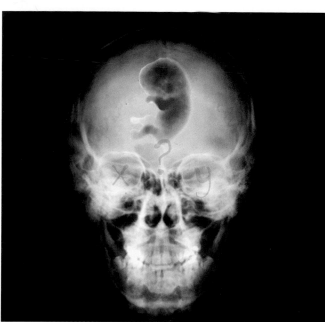

Skull X-ray (left)
Media artist Simon Kavanagh made this X-ray image in response to worrying speculation that parents may soon be able to genetically design their own babies.

Superdry X-ray ad (below)
In this campaign for Superdry created by photographer Sam Clifford-Harding a gritty street shot of a worker wearing a canvas bag is juxtaposed with an X-ray security image showing its rugged construction.

DIY
Use X-rays and other medical technology such as MRI (magnetic resonance imaging) scans, ultrasound scans and full body scanners to disclose an inner or unexpected truth, thought or secret.

Brainjack
X-rays are highly graphic and can compellingly reveal the hidden or unexpected.

Y

You! (put yourself in it)

Tim Walker
Walker's stunning fashion photographs have enchanted readers of British and Italian *Vogue* for over a decade. His pictures are wonderfully idiosyncratic and uniquely his own, imprinted with his passions, obsessions, memories and influences and filled with his love of crumbling country houses, historic fashion photos, old movies and fairytales. Here he takes inspiration from Hans Christian Andersen's The Princess and The Pea. *See* www.timwalkerphotography.com

Express yourself. What is your personal heritage? Put your attitudes into your work. Rewrite your own history. What is personal to you in a brief? Find a link between your experience and your work. Every day, record objects or happenings you find remarkable, or that seem too good to be true. Others may share your excitement. Be true to yourself; be heartfelt. Imprint your work with your personal vision. Put your stamp on it. Create something you love – others may also love it. See Finding ideas.

'*Derive ideas from your experience, from the world around you, from your own background, from your childhood, from relationships with others, from the social and political environment. Don't be confined to a pond… in which the water is always in danger of becoming stagnant.*'
Ken Garland, graphic designer

Z

Zeitgeist

An idea doesn't have to be timeless. It has to work now. It must capture the zeitgeist, a German word that describes the spirit of a specific time or period. The 1920s was the jazz age, the 1950s the jet age, the 1960s the space age and the start of the 21st century was the bling age, characterized by Martin Parr's photographcs of Russian oligarchs and Damien Hirst's use of diamonds and 18-carat gold in his sculptures. Spot the age you are living in now.

Wang Tiande, *Tiande Investments: Art Index LED*, 2008 (above)
Chinese artist Wang Tiande captured the zeitgeist of 2008 in this gallery installation. The spirit of the time was one of global fear of economic meltdown and of imminent economic crash and visitors sat mesmerized as minute by minute a live feed of share prices fluctuated on a massive stock market LED screen. Strangely beautiful, the flickering coloured lights created the profile of the mountains and valleys seen in traditional Chinese painting.

'*The Pop artists spotted that if the seventeenth century had been all about saints then the 1960s was the decade of pop stars and film stars.*'
Emma Wright, journalist

'*Be a weathervane for the new.*'
Rose Tang, artist

DIY
Feel the pulse of the now. Divine your times. Connect to the now and the new. Saturate yourself in contemporary culture. What are the latest developments – globally, nationally and locally?

Make the way you execute your idea 'of the now'. Why make the present seem second-hand by using the styles of the past?

Brainjack
An idea inspired by the zeitgeist connects to viewers by making sense of what is happening now. It gives them a feeling of inclusion because they have spotted and understood something that reflects the spirit of the age.

Index

Picture credits

10 *John Ingledew*
11 *Private collection, London*
12–13 *Courtesy and © Kirsty Pook*
14 *Courtesy and © Jimmy Turrell*
25 *Courtesy and © Kirsty Pook*
26 *Courtesy WDMP*
27 *E. J. Major, Venus Vanitas, 2009 C-type print, 117 x 97cm. Image courtesy of Salon Contemporary – www.saloncontemporary.com*
28 tl *Courtesy Fabrica*
28tr *Courtesy and © Red Saunders*
28b *Courtesy and © Dick Jewell*
29 *The Way Home, 2000 courtesy the artist Tom Hunter*
30tl *Ruth Adams*
30bl *David Pearson/Courtesy and © Penguin Books*
30r *Courtesy and © Ian Wright*
31tl *Library of Congress*
31r *Marcus Harvey, Myra, 1995, Acrylic on canvas, 156 x 126in. © the artist. Photo: Stephen White. Courtesy White Cube*
31bl *Invader, Rubik London Calling 2009. Image courtesy Jonathan LeVine Gallery*
32 *Private collection, London*
33 *Private collection, London*
34 *Thatcha! Ten Years of the Dragon, 1989. Reproduced courtesy of Spitting Image*
35l *Courtesy Jonathan Barnbrook*
35r *Ben Cannon*
36 *Courtesy Januzzi Smith*
37b *Courtesy Jamie Dobson*
38 *Courtesy Aboud Creative © Paul Smith, photography © David Bailey*
39r *Heat Wave electric radiator for Droog by Joris Laarman. Photo by Robaard/Theuwkens (Styling by Marjo Kranenborg, CMK)*
40 *Courtesy: Galerie Bruno Bischofberger, Zurich & Tony Shafrazi Gallery, New York*
41 *Courtesy Aboud Creative © Paul Smith, photography © Hugh Hales-Tooke*
42 tl and cl *Courtesy Dave Stokes*
42 cr (lovehearts) *courtesy Nicole Davies*
42b *Client: Royal Academy of Arts. Design: Why Not Associates*
43 t *Yang Yongliang, Phantom Landscape II No. 2, 2006. © the artist*
43 bl *Photograph John Ingledew*
43 br *Courtesy FABRICA*
44l *Wallpaper*, August 2009. © Neville Brody and Wallpaper* Magazine 2009*
44r *Courtesy Webb and Webb Design*
45 *Courtesy Tom Ford*
46tl *Moving Brands (photography and creative)*
46bl *Courtesy Design Act*
46r *Hussein Chalayan, A/W07 'Airborne' collection. In collaboration with Swarovski. © Chris Moore*
47 *Body Paint by Mehmet Akten. http://www.msavisuals.com/body_paint*
48 *Courtesy Ron Arad Associates*
49 tl *Courtesy Thomas Charvériat/ISland6, © Lui Dao*
49 bl *Photographs John Ingledew*
49br *Photographs courtesy Geoff Putnam*
50-51 *Photographs © Joanna Kane, with thanks for permission for photography from the Scottish National Portrait Gallery and the William Ramsay Henderson Trust*
52 *Department of Health, Tobacco Control (2007). Miles Calcraft Briginshaw Duffy, London. Photo: Nick Georghiou*
53 *Private collection, London*
54 *John Ingledew*
55t *Private collection, London*
55b *Agency: BMP. Courtesy DDB UK*
56tl *Jon Allan/I KP*

56tr *Courtesy Swarovski Elements. Photo: Nick Knight*
56b *Courtesy Fabrica*
57t *Art Direction: Takuya Onuki. Client: Laforet, Tokyo*
57bl *Courtesy Wolff Olins*
57br *John Ingledew*
58t *Kieran Hunt, www.kieranhunt.com*
58bl *Courtesy and © Jimmy Turrell*
58 br *Courtesy and © Samantha Bourne and Kelly Morse*
59 *AOI Images 34 Call for Entries Card, illustration by Frazer Hudson (initially commissioned by The Guardian, 2009)*
60 *Courtesy Copper Greene*
61t *Courtesy Wing Design*
61b *Design and Production GRP Glasgow. Client: NHS Ayrshire and Arran, Lanarkshire and Greater Glasgow and Clyde*
62 *Courtesy and © Andy Freeberg*
63 *All John Ingledew*
64t *Courtesy and © Nike*
64b *Bartle Bogle Hegarty. Image courtesy The National Union of Students*
65 *Courtesy Liu Yizhong*
66 *Courtesy Pete Bedwell and Louis Mason*
67tl *Courtesy Christoph Niemann*
67tr *French Market Poster Design by Alistair Hall at We Made This LTD, client: Brent Council, www.wemadethis.co.uk*
67br *© Penguin Books*
68l *Courtesy Jonathan Barnbrook*
68r *Courtesy Martino Gamper*
69l *Image courtesy Martin J. Walker/Reproduced in Hornsey 1968, The Art School Revolution, by Lisa Tickner. Frances Lincoln Limited © 2008*
69r *Courtesy Mark Perry*
70l *Atelier Populaire*
70r *Courtesy Tony Moon*
71 *Design: johnson banks, Designers: Michael Johnson, Pal Palavathanan*
72 *Museum für Gestaltung Zürich, Poster Collection, Franz Xaver Jaggy © ZHdK*
73l *Courtesy Peter Kennard*
73r *Private collection, Cape Town*
74t *Design: johnson banks, Designers: Michael Johnson, Kath Tudball*
74b *John Ingledew*
75 *Courtesy Leanne Newcombe*
76 *© V&A Images, Victoria and Albert Museum*
77 *Courtesy Ron Arad Associates*
78 *Courtesy and © Margaux Luzuriaga*
80 *Photograph by JI, © Liou Ming Law*
81 *Laura Moody, Zoe Shannon, model: Louis Mason*
82tl and bl *TBWA/Chiat/Day. © 1997 Apple Computer, Inc. All Rights Reserved*
82br *Courtesy DDB Worldwide, New York*
83 *The Ronald Grant Archive/Channel Four Films*
84 *Simon Patterson, The Great Bear, 1992, 109.2 x 134.6 cm, 4-colour lithograph in glass and aluminium frame. Edition of 50. Copyright Simon Patterson and Transport for London. Photograph Stephen White, Courtesy Haunch of Venison*
85t *Courtesy Shortlist Media Limited*
85 bl and br *Photography John Ingledew*
86 *Private collection, London*
87 *Bridget Riley, Blaze 4, 1963. Emulsion on board. 109 x 109 cm. Private Collection. © Bridget Riley 2010. All Rights Reserved. Courtesy Karsten Schubert*
88 *© and Courtesy Shigeo Fukuda Studio*
89t *Courtesy Calum Colville. www.calumcolvin.com*
89bl *Courtesy David Pearson*
89br *Courtesy Lloyds Bank*
90–91 *How to Be a Fashion Photographer courtesy DIESEL*

156b Photography by Alan Mahon
157 Photography John Ingledew
158t squid london, www.squidlondon.com, co-founders and directors Emma-Jayne Parkes and Viviane Jaeger
158b Photos courtesy Trudie Ballantyne
159 Courtesy and © Gerald Scarfe
160l Courtesy D&AD
160r Courtesy Marketing Birmingham
161 Courtesy Jon Quinnell
162–63 courtesy Thomas Charvériat/Island6 © Lui Dao
164 Real Life is Rubbish, 2002. © Tim Noble & Sue Webster. Image courtesy of the artists
165b Charles Deering McCormick Library of Special Collections, Northwestern University Library, Illinois
165t Courtesy Broken Hearts, illustration: Rob Flowers, photography Ian Bonhote, clothes: Broken Hearts for Beyond the Valley, shoes: Terry de Havilland Couture
166 © and Courtesy Shigeo Fukuda Studio
167t Ogilvy & Mather Advertising Beijing. Creative Director: Wilson Chow, Art Director: Hui Ru He, Copywriter: Wilson Chow, Photographer Riggs Lau
167b Courtesy CDP. Creative team: Mike Cozens and Alan Waldie/ Photographer: Brian Duffy.
168 Courtesy Sécurité Routière
169l With kind permission of Barnardo's and BBH photographer Nick Georghiou
169tr Design/Typography – The Designers Republic. Image – Chris Cunningham
169br Courtesy Peter Saville
170–71 John Ingledew
172 Courtesy Rob Ryan
173 Photography John Ingledew
174 © The Estate of Joseph Binder
175l Photography John Ingledew
175tr Courtesy Rose Tang/Island6
176–77 Courtesy Alan Latchley, Emma D'Arcy, Amber Newland, Jay Dolves, Lucie Beardwood, Mark Lavery
178 Courtesy Pierre et Gilles
179t Courtesy Hemingway Studio
179b Courtesy Aboud Creative © Paul Smith
180 Image courtesy Kartell (www.kartell.it)
181 Courtesy and © David Abrahams
182 Surprise Milan – art direction: Diego Paccagnella; concept and design: Jonas Lund – Thorbjørn Ankerstjerne; company Lago s.p.a Italy
183l © Penguin Books
183r Private collection, London
184 Courtesy Channel 4
185 © Guardian News and Media Limited 2010
186 The Ronald Grant Archive
187 Simon Kavanagh mediartist
188t Courtesy JWT, London
188b Courtesy Jonathan Barnbrook
189tl Library of Congress
189tr Private Collection, London
189b BMP Davidson Pearce
190 Courtesy and © Nick Meers
191–92 John Ingledew
193 Courtesy Nick Pride
194l Exclamation Mark. Art Director - Ned Corbett-Winder, Copy Writer - Martin Latham, Graphic/Designer - Gareth Davies, Producer - Ray Price. M&C Saatchi, London
194r DM9 DDB Publicidade, Sao Paulo
195 Courtesy Jonathan Barnbrook

196tl Courtesy Jimmy Turrell
196tr Jung von Matt/basis GmbH/Angela Hoch
196bl RKCR/Y&R, London
196br © Rene Clement/Polaris/Eyevine
197 Courtesy The Chase
198–99 All photography John Ingledew
200t Keep Playing. Creative Director: Maurizio Cinti, Art Director: Sergio Lelli/Andrea Ligi, Copy Writer Silva Fedrigo/Rebecca Rossi, Account Supervisor: Emiliana Palazzi/Elisabetta Santagata, Photo: AdmCom
200b More Time for Children. Boebel/Adam Werbeagentur, Frankfurt. Photo Jens Görlich
201 Ken Garland
202 John Ingledew
203 Photograph by Alex So, thanks to Kate Vincent-Smith © Converse
204–05 illy world tour, author: Diego Paccagnella
206l Lowe Howard-Spink, UK
206r Abbott Mead Vickers. BBDO, London
207 Courtesy Jonathan Barnbrook
208 John Heartfield, Adolf the Superman Swallows Gold and Talks Tinplate, 1932. Private Collection, London/© The Heartfield Community of Heirs/ VG Bild-Kunst, Bonn and DACS, London 2011
209t Courtesy Simon Kavanagh
209b Courtesy Sam Clifford-Harding
210 Courtesy Tim Walker, thanks to Alison Tanner and Polly Penrose
211 © Wang Tiande Studio

Jacket photograph: Nathan Hager

Acknowledgements

Thanks to Jo Lightfoot who commissioned this book, Peter Jones who edited it, Peter Kent for his excellent gathering of pictures and Jessie Earle for the design.

Many thanks are also due to the following people for their invaluable contributions to this book: Ken Garland, Joe Boylan, Chris J Bailey, Thomas Charvériat, Trudie Ballantyne, Nick Meers, Hong Xixu, John Brewer, Red Saunders, Ian Wright, Calum Colvin, Joanna Kane, Simon Kavanagh, Julie Zhu YuMei, Ross Cooper, Neil Aitkin, Phil Baines, David Pearson, Alistair Hall, Michele Jannuzzi, Tom Hunter, Rose Tang, Dan Knight, Kathy Prendergast, Lisa Rienermann, Alan Aboud, Hugh Hales-Tooke, David Bailey, Minnie Weisz, E. J. Major, Robert Stadler, Nick Knight, Gregory Crewdson, Tim Walker, Alison Tanner, Polly Penrose, Nadav Kander, Zoe Tomlinson, Gavin Bond, Nicolai Howalt, Andy Freeberg, Nick Hastings, Liam Gibson, Jon Gledstone, Jon Mitchell, Georg Thesmann, Dick Jewell, Martino Gamper, Tony Moon, Mark Perry, Invader, Jimmy Turrell, Margaux Luzuriaga, Stefanie Posavec, David McCandless, Alex Shields, William Eckersley, Jamie Dobson, Yuxing Gong, Bohnchang Koo, Wang Tiande, Yang Yongliang, David Abrahams, Matt Walford, Julian Woollams, Kath Tudball, Miho Aishima, Michael Johnson, Pali Palavathanan, James Bull, Ben Wolstenholme, Georgina Milne, Mike Heath, Rebecca Brown, Zoe Sinclair, Andrea Blood, Thea Swayne, Selina Swayne, Graeme Raeburn, Sara Carneholm, Diego Paccagnella, Omar Vulpinari, Barbara Liverotti, Rob Ryan, Hazel Nicholls, Katie Montgomery, Emma- Jayne Parkes, Viviane Jaeger, Nisha Thirkell, Amber Jane Butchart, Ian Bonhole, Rob Flowers, Joss McKinley, Dan Stafford, Nick Pride, Tim Adams, Adam Stinson, Frank Holmes, Stuart Wilding, Richard Billingham, Paul Boon, Clive Barrett, Sharon Harper, Emma Hughes, Matt Frederick, Gary Jones Slater, Andy Tibbs, Kieran Phelps, Annabel Jeffrey, Roger Puplett, David Thompson, Andy Godwin, Ben Cannon, Kieran Hunt, Cleon Daniel, Lauren Mitton, Ruth Adams, Dave Stokes, Leah Evans, Jacob Russell, Lizzie Ayre, Leanne Newcombe, Hannah Farmer, Laura Moody, Zoe Shannon, Pete Bedwell, Louis Mason, Sam Clifford-Harding, Joe Currie, David Swailes, Jono Smithies, Christina Barrett, Kayleigh J. Moore, Jim Brook, Dan Hirst, James Crickmore, Oliver Wenman, Maddie Page, Nicole Vernon, Kirsty Pook, Will Folet, Samantha Bourne and Kelly Morse, Emma D'Arcy, Amber Newland, Jay Delves, Lucie Beardwood, Mark Lavery, Jon Quinnell, Dan Ford, Schway Whar, Geoff Putnam, Mowfak Galy, Dean Menezes, Itamar Medeiros, Martin Kettlewell, Annie Morrad, Jorge Otero, Arnaud Marquoin-Seignolles, Andy Lawrence, Phil Dorman, Christer Windeløv-Lidzélius, Dennis Dybda and Espen Sivertsen.

Thanks also to the following supporters, collaborators, consigliere and inspirations: Nigel Langford, Kevin Jones, Kate Vincent-Smith, Tim Marshall, Dave Hendley, Andy Haslam, Dan Alexander, Andrew Foster, Geoff Fowle, Andrew Whittle, Richard Doust, Maz Raein, Mac McAuley, Val Palmer, Marcus Bastel, Clive Challis, Sandro Sodano, Steve Harries, Mel Bles, Stuart Selner, Jon Whitelock, Mark Ingledew, Lee Widdows, James Langdon-Davies, John Palmer, Tom Greenhalgh, John Langford, Julz Sale, Randy Seewald, Deborah Hardingham, John Stephen Fink, Alan Latchley, Franco Di Lauro, Edgar Snow, Colin Jones, Roger Gwatkin, Blaise Douglas, Steve Pyke, Lorentz Gullachsen, Mark Guthrie, Gino Sprio, Hygin Kibuanda, Guy Scott Thomas, Ryan Herman, Alex Leith, Clive Batty, Francis Glibbery, Jack Birney, Steve Pyke, Charlie Ward, Arthur Miller, Ronnie Wycherley and Alan Hudson.

This book was written with the support of a research grant from the University of Gloucestershire.

Dedication
For D.R., O. and D.

E.S.I.

p g a t p